RADICAL
REINVENTION

RADICAL
REINVENTION

AN

UNLIKELY

RETURN

TO THE

CATHOLIC

CHURCH

KAYA OAKES

COUNTERPOINT · BERKELEY, CALIFORNIA

Copyright © 2012 Kaya Oakes

Author's note: Names and descriptions of individuals have been changed throughout the book. Place names have occasionally been changed as well. Events are in the best chronological order that the author is able to recall, but her recall is occasionally not that great. *Omnia in tempore Dei.* And no, the author's Latin is not that great either.

Library of Congress Cataloging-in-Publication Data is available.

ISBN: 978-1-59376-431-9

Cover design by Elke Barter
Interior design by Neuwirth & Associates, Inc.

COUNTERPOINT
1919 Fifth Street
Berkeley, CA 94710
Printed in the United States of America
Distributed by Publishers Group West

10 9 8 7 6 5 4 3 2 1

A man walks into a monastery and says, "I want to be a monk."

The abbot replies, "Great! But you realize we're only allowed to talk every ten years."

The man replies, "Fine."

Ten years go by and the man goes into the abbot's office. The abbot asks, "Well, my son, what have you to say?"

The man replies, "Bed's hard."

The abbot remarks, "Is that it?"

The man says, "Yes."

Another ten years go by and the man goes into the abbot's office and says, "Food stinks!"

The abbot asks, "Is that it?"

And the man says, "Yes."

Another ten years go by and the man goes into the abbot's office and says, "Water's cold. I quit!"

And the abbot replies, "Figures! You've been complaining ever since you got here!"

—Source unknown

RADICAL
REINVENTION

PROLOGUE

PROLOGUE

Hell was revealed to me the day I got busted for drawing on my hand with a Magic Marker. An eighth-grader supervised as I scrubbed my hand in the sink during detention. "I swear to God," I told this thin-faced blonde, "I didn't mean anything bad."

"Do you know what happens when you say 'I swear to God'?" she asked.

I shook my head. I was seven, maybe eight years old.

"When you die, you go straight to Hell."

It was the 1970s and the elderly nuns at my Catholic school no longer wore habits. A group of Moonies had moved into the building next door, which used to be the nuns' convent when their numbers were higher. Now there were only a few of them left and they shared a small apartment around the block. We were admonished never to speak to the Moonies, who offered us candy during recess. But I was a rotten-toothed candy addict and found it hard to say no to those perpetually smiling Moonies.

"Do you know what happens if you say 'I swear to the Holy Spirit'?" the eighth grader continued.

Had Mom and Dad ever mentioned this? Dad was always saying "I swear to God." He also said "shit," "Jesus fucking Christ," "goddamn," "hell," "fuck," and "dammit," sometimes all squashed together after he'd drunk enough wine: "shitfuckgoddamnjesuschristhell." What did any of this have to do with the Holy Spirit? The eighth grader leaned closer, looking into my eyes.

"If you ever say 'I swear to the Holy Spirit,'" she said, pointing at my face, "you'll go straight to Hell without even dying first."

After detention, I walked home, reached over the fence for the house key, let myself in, walked upstairs to my room, knelt on the floor, and whispered, "I swear to the Holy Spirit." Highly suspicious of her theory, I wanted some empirical evidence to prove that she was right. Nothing happened, unless I've been in Hell ever since.

A couple of weeks after that detention, one of the nuns told us a story. A little boy was sick and on the verge of death. She showed us a pastel sketch of a red-cheeked, blond boy in a pristine white nightshirt, his eyes rolled toward Heaven. He was just about to die when he called out to Jesus to save him. Jesus came in a white robe and laid his hand on the boy's face. The boy lived.

"Anytime you call out to Jesus, when you're in danger, he will come and save you," the nun said.

Recess arrived and I looked down at the asphalt of the playground. Then I took off my glasses, folded them up, and placed them on the ground. I backed up a few paces and broke into a hard sprint. After I'd gotten up as much speed as my chunky legs could manage, I flung myself hard at a swath of asphalt, and, like the dying kid, called out to Jesus. That day, I walked home with brown blood crusting my pebbly wounds. Clearly, I was going to Hell. It must have been the marker.

Jesus didn't give a shit about fat little girls with rat's nests in their hair who slept in dirty T-shirts and drew on their hands. So I became fatter, dirtier, and louder. I answered every rhetorical question in catechism with a sarcastic remark, refused to pray, and rolled my eyes so hard during Mass that people probably thought I was an epileptic. At the end of the school year, my mother insisted that I start attending a public school. The teacher there was an arty single mother who wore aprons and had us throwing pottery in the back of the classroom when we got out of control. Nobody ever talked about God.

The Catholic Church I grew up in may have had its share of Hell, primarily in the form of batshit eighth-grade detention monitors, but it also held an appeal for a fourth-generation Bay Area girl. I was born in 1971, and thus am a child of a decade that began in radicalism and ended on the verge of Reaganomics. Vatican II ended in 1965, ushering in a new era in the Church: ecumenicism, a new sense of openness between clergy and laypeople, hopes for more progressive reform, and most importantly, Mass in the vernacular instead of Latin.

My Catholic elementary school grappled with the reforms of Vatican II. Although the nuns were pleased to be walking around out of habits, they were awkward in normal clothes. With cropped haircuts, polyester skirt suits grazing their knees, and small crosses hanging around their necks, they looked like peppy grandmothers. In religious studies class, for lack of instructions from the Vatican about new forms of catechism, we made endless God's eyes, wrapping yarn around popsicle sticks and carrying them home to mothers who already had a line of God's eyes on the windowsill from the previous week's classes. We crafted tissue-paper collages about Jesus and did skits about saints that often involved someone being martyred for extra credit. My older sister's high school performed *Godspell* and *Jesus Christ Superstar*, and after that I believed that Jesus really wore bell-bottoms and a Superman shirt. Catholicism was a lot of things in the 1970s, but from my preadolescent perspective, it was mostly entertaining and slightly absurd.

But the Catholic Church I grew up in was not just about clunky tradition and occasionally dorky catechism: it was about service to others, liberation theology, and the legacy of scholarship used to enlighten the present day. As a child, I never heard Latin in Mass, not even when the priest said the blessing at communion, or sang songs other than the folky hymns that were popularized by groups like the St. Louis Jesuits, authors of tunes like the soft rock "Earthen Vessels," which we crooned to the accompaniment of an acoustic guitar. When I made my first confession, instead of heading into a dim closet and sitting behind a screen, I sat in a folding chair on the altar, face to face with the priest, while my classmates giggled and poked one another far back in the pews. It was an experiment called "open confession," and in my case it totally failed: freaked out with the stage fright that would plague me for the rest of my life, I started bawling and ran out of the church as soon as the priest asked what my sins had been. But the priest came and found me, apologized for the entire experiment, and excused me from open confession from then on.

My education veered between Catholic grammar school and public elementary school, Catholic high school and alternative learning high school, experimental public college and Catholic college, public graduate school and Catholic graduate school. The Catholic college was mostly a matter of money: my father worked there, and tuition was free. The other changes were based on my teacher-mother's attempt to find other good teachers. But all that back and forth meant I was religiously half-baked. There was catechism in the sense that religious talk happened, but a lot of it consisted of overheard conversations between my dad and the Christian Brothers he worked with, who came over to drink and debate philosophy in our living room. There was the Catholic church we attended, but it was a very Bay Area kind of place, with folk Mass and liturgical dance, occasional reflections by female parishioners, and late night Mass in the dark. There was an early exodus within our ranks: my mother got sick of the ritual and stopped attending Mass, and soon stopped advocating for the latter end of her five kids to attend Catholic school, which is when my younger sister and I began bouncing around. My father worked for a Catholic school in the suburbs; my mother worked for the public schools in Oakland, where we lived. But even though I was assured by priests and nuns that my baptism made me a Catholic for life, nobody was ever able to explain what being a Catholic really meant. And the one person who might have explained it best to me exited the picture before I knew how to ask the right questions.

In 1989, when I was eighteen, my father crashed his VW van on the way to work. He spent three months in the ICU, thrashing and hallucinating with alcoholic DTs and brain trauma, but he seemed to be on the mend by the time I boarded a Greyhound bus for an overnight ride to Olympia, where I'd be attending an artsy alternative college. I saw him briefly at Christmas and he'd transformed from a bear into a wraith: suddenly, he was white-haired and spectrally thin, like something out of a horror film. He died in his sleep one night soon after the New Year.

The funeral was the first Catholic Mass I'd been to in years. As an adolescent I'd occasionally gone to twilight Mass on Sundays, with just a guitar for music and near-darkness except for a few candles. It was the kind of Catholic ceremony I secretly enjoyed, but eventually hormones took over and I blew Dad off when he asked if I'd go along. Instead I sat in my room, listening to the Replacements and scratching out agonized poems to boys who ignored me.

In contrast to the intimate environment of weekly Mass, his funeral was crowded, loud, and brightly lit, with oppressive organ music raining down from a balcony crammed with pipes, speeches by his Christian Brother colleagues in their black cassocks and white bibs, and a reception afterward where I shook hands with people I'd never met before, all of whom wanted to tell some sort of story about my funny, angry, impatient, complicated father.

Dad was an only child born when his parents were nearly forty, and they raised him in an area of West Oakland crammed full of poor Irish. His own father was a dancing-on-tables sort of drunk. One evening, he danced right off a table and collapsed onto the floor, sending my grandmother into panicked early labor. Dad was tiny and not expected to make it. He did. Everyone had prayed. He was Catholic to the bone, despite his constant swearing, often taking the Lord's name in vain in surprisingly creative ways (I can still hear him saying "holy bitch tits fucking virgin" over a flat tire), and in spite of his itinerant habit of taking off and leaving us for weeks at a stretch while he pursued a solitude that was lost to him once his five children were born.

After his funeral Mass, I didn't set foot in a church for nearly a decade. But as much as I subsumed myself in secular (and clearly illegal) activities with too many sulky, disaffected men and boys, somehow I was always being pulled back to prayer. When I was in the back of a car being driven by a very drunk guy and we slammed into a tree, the words out of my mouth were "Oh, God, please don't." I walked away with a sprained hand, and my boyfriend at the time laughed about my holy interjection for months. During a mushroom trip in another boyfriend's apartment, a corona of flames flickered around his head, and I mumbled, "Holy Spirit set you on fire . . . dude" before running off to the bathroom to retch. I developed a habit of crossing myself whenever I saw a cat or dog crushed on the road. All the guys I've dated have been atheists, and needless to say, they found my holy inclinations annoying. But for me, there's something irresistibly sexy about unbelievers, since it requires such high self-esteem to reject the idea of God altogether. Sartre once said that if God existed, he couldn't, and if he existed, God couldn't. If confidence is sex, Sartre must have been the George Clooney of philosophy.

Maybe it's just in my genes. Vesicular monamine transporter 2 is a protein found in every human body. In some people, it results in a greater sense of what a psychiatrist named C. Robert Cloninger refers to as self-transcendence: a willingness to believe in things that can't be objectively proven. A geneticist named Dean Hamer links this to heredity. If one or both of your parents believed in God, it's more likely that you will believe in God too. When I read about this so-called God gene, a bell went off inside my skull. Maybe my tendency to fall into contemplative states pondering the nature of creation was something I'd inherited and not the result of a few bong hits. Maybe there really was a God. Maybe I occasionally snuck into a Catholic Mass because my genes wanted me to go. Or maybe it was just another way of being different; after all, Generation X has the highest percentage of self-identified atheists and agnostics in recent history. If my earlier years had meant rebellion via punk rock, a shaved head, and tattoos, my nascent rediscovery of faith seemed rebellious in contrast to my aging hip peers who seemed to take pride in their atheism. Or maybe, in spite of my politics, which only became more progressive as I got older, the Catholic Church just felt like my spiritual home.

For several years in my early thirties, I attended Christmas Eve midnight Mass at Saint Joseph the Worker, a large, primarily Chicano parish in the West Berkeley neighborhood where I used to live. The pastor was a big-bellied left-wing Irish American named Father Bill O'Donnell, who'd successfully changed the name of the parish from "Workman" to "Worker" as a nod to his female parishioners. When he wasn't serving Masses or running the parish, Father Bill was getting arrested—nearly 250 times—for protesting torture, war, and U.S. military schools. In the 1970s, he'd marched with Cesar Chavez in the farm workers' rights movement. During the intercessions, he croaked out, in a voice hoarse from shouting at protests, "Let us pray for the ordination of women." My soul leapt a little with the hope that here was the kind of priest I could handle, but then he died from a massive heart attack. I could have given up at that point. Even in the Bay Area, it is not easy to find a liberal-leaning Catholic church. And to be honest, I'd picked just about the worst time in recent history to go looking for the church I'd grown up in.

With the election of Pope Benedict XVI in 2005, the Vatican was getting more and more vocal about the so-called evils of birth control and abortion, and as a lifelong feminist who'd depended on Planned Parenthood for medical care in my pre-insurance years, this was an obvious problem. Likewise, the fact that I grew up surrounded by and loving the gay community meant that the "love the sinner, hate the sin" edict issued by the prior pope was a problem as well. Benedict spoke out against distributing condoms in AIDS-ravaged African countries; he urged parishes to offer the archaic Latin Rite Mass and tinkered with the Roman Rite to bring the translation closer to the original, even if it sounded like shit in English; Holocaust-denying bishops who had been stripped of their titles were reinstated because, according to Benedict, they had "repented"; sexual abuse cases were repeatedly swept under the rug. As my mother put it, "A *German* pope? What the hell were they thinking?" Like the empathy I felt for the people who wanted to leave the country when Bush was elected and re-elected, I understood why millions of people were fleeing the Church. But just as I argued that it was better to stay in the United States and resist the regime from within, I secretly began to believe the same thing about

Catholicism. Would it ever have any hope of changing if people like me bailed on it?

Over the years, I've wondered if, rather than rejoining this troubled, troubling institution, I ought to look for a church that's closer to my political beliefs, something like the Episcopalians or the United Church of Christ, both of which not only have female clergy but support gay people as well. But there's a root problem: I'm Irish, and when you're an Irish Catholic, even a radical one, some part of you is always going to be Catholic. It's that God gene, but it's also the narrative I was brought up with, the story that we were part of an oppressed minority that came to America fleeing oppression and found . . . more oppression. There's something appealing about the idea that my ancestors were not tea-sipping Episcopalian Wasps, but broke-as-hell, ghetto-dwelling, hard-swearing, garbage-truck-driving, potato-famine-escaping, gallon-o'-whiskey-drinking, short-lifespan living Catholics. Yes, the Irish Catholic Church has even more ills to answer for than the American Church, but it's also part of my culture. When I pray, I know generations of my family who came before me prayed in the very same way.

And there was something else I found out from visiting services in other denominations: the feeling is not the same. The local Episcopalians bored me with their uninspiring sermons. Sure, they had the awesome openly gay bishop Gene Robinson on their side, but the endless repetition of every verse in the hymns was yawn-inducing. The United Church of Christ people had some embarrassing white-people hip-shaking thing at their service that reminded me why I never dance in public. Praying with the Unitarians felt like entering a vacuum. I couldn't deal with the awkward silence of the Quakers. Meditation was fine, but for me Buddhism itself lacked anything to work toward, other than nothingness.

The fact of the matter is that I was only shopping and playing fake atheist to avoid one thing: confronting and trying to make peace with the Church I'd left behind. Some arcane part of me pined for Catholicism even as I ground my teeth every time another horrible story about it emerged in the news. The Greeks referred to a deep, visceral kind of longing as *splangchnizomai*, *splangcha* being their term for "guts." In the Epistle to the Philippians, Paul writes that he misses his community "in the *splangcha* of Christ." That's where I missed Catholicism, the feeling it gave me to pray, and to pray with others: deep in my guts. For better or worse, I loved the mystery of it, the rituals that had been repeated millions of times over thousands of years by billions of people around the world. If coming back to the Church meant I was destined to be a cafeteria Catholic, oh well. When you eat in a cafeteria, you stick to the tastiest foods and walk right by the congealing, nasty, old-looking stuff. Screw the dogma, I figured. I'm Catholic in my guts. Let's just deal with that.

Father Mellow's office is a cramped, shadowy room on the second floor of my childhood church. The walls are cluttered with photos and icons, and bookshelves are squeezed together in every available space. A Tibetan prayer flag flutters above the hissing gas heater. There's no fire and brimstone about this nearly ninety-year-old priest; he is the most chilled-out person I've ever met. Later I will read an anecdote about people who have been in holy orders for most of their lives, how they face the waning years with a sense of gladness, not fear. It's the opposite of the anxiety-prone, panic-riddled condition I seem to inhabit, and even from the first moments of our conversation, I drink it up like a woman plucked from the desert. He folds his hands and looks me in the eye, asking, "So, what's your story? What brings you here?" For the first time in quite a while, I lack an answer. I'm a teacher, and midway through most of my classes I'll find myself barreling off-topic from whatever text we're discussing and launching into an anecdote from my own life. Maybe it's narcissism, but most of the shrinks I've consulted over the years have instead labeled it with other names: anxiety, introversion, low self-esteem. I talk a good talk to cover up how pathetic and awkward other people make me feel. Suddenly, however, there's no answer for this calm, blue-eyed old man. "I was raised Catholic," I begin, after a pause, "but it stopped mattering . . ." He nods and waits. Try again. "I'm a writer"—lamest excuse in the book, lady, and don't you dare swear—"and I've been around atheists and agnostics for a long time, and I got tired of pretending I don't believe in God." He nods again and asks, "So what do you want to do about that?" I realize that he is beholding me, but not in the way people usually behold me. It's not that I'm especially attractive, but I am so used to being judged for my appearance, it's hard to understand someone might be looking at me and thinking about my soul.

It would be nice to say at that very moment I shouted "I want to BELIEVE" and we raced downstairs to the chapel, where I was washed in the waters of the font. However, this is not a story of being born again; if I wanted to be an evangelical I could just hop into a church and they'd dip me in a tub and serve me cake. I'd been dipped already anyway—I was two months old, wore a satin christening gown, and am told I took it with eyes open and did not cry. But I shook off that baptismal water many times, and I can't just walk back in and let it rain down on me again.

I've read the stories of Catholic converts—smart, saintly people like Thomas Merton and Dorothy Day—and many of them swallowed the faith whole, like a Eucharistic host. But if you were born into it and left by choice, faith tends to stick to the back of your throat. Catholics don't make it easy to join up or come back. Sure, Jesus was able to amble up to John the Baptist and be plunged into the Jordan, but he's Jesus. Obviously, I am not. During Vatican II, the church realized that it needed to re-evaluate the process by which adults were received into the Church. Jesus told the apostles that they should teach those who were drawn to his ministry, but over the years a distinct series of steps toward adult baptism or confirmation had never been formally established. So in 1963, the cardinals wrote that "the catechumenate for adults, comprising several distinct steps, is to be restored and to be taken into use," and by 1972 the Rite of Christian Initiation for Adults (RCIA) had emerged.

In the primitive church, catechumens (those waiting to be

baptized) were treated like second-class citizens. They were allowed to attend the first part of the Mass, but were shooed away before the Eucharist. In some churches they even had to enter through a side door, and many had to wait decades before they were welcomed into the church. Saint Augustine was made a catechumen while he was an infant, but he wasn't baptized until he was in his thirties, and in between he got into a lot of fascinating messes. His prayer in the intervening years was, famously, "Grant me chastity and continence . . . but not yet." Wanting to avoid getting into this kind of potentially corrupting delay with other converts, the Vatican came up with a programmed series of classes, rituals, and ceremonies to help people understand what they were getting into by becoming Catholic.

Many of the people who begin RCIA are brand-new to Catholicism and know nothing about it; others are marrying Catholics and have to convert to be married in a church; and others, like me, had a bit of it as kids but were never confirmed, which is supposed to give you the gifts of the Holy Spirit and make your relationship with God stronger. As the religion has been around for about two millennia, there's a lot of ground to cover, and RCIA usually starts in the fall and ends at Easter, its weekly meetings filling the better part of the calendar year. "We start with God and Mary and Jesus," Father Mellow tells me in his office, "the general stuff. You've already got that, right?" Nod. "In the spring we move on to the sacraments, Catholic life, and so on. It's December now, but you've already been baptized, so you could join us when we start up again in January and see what you think."

So I plan to go back to the Church in January. People have been dying all around me: grandparents, mother-in-law, several friends. After eleven years together, my husband and I may as well be living on separate continents. I'm at the tail end of publishing a book that has caused me to pack on thirty pounds of stress-induced weight, constant anxiety means the underarms of my shirts are always dark with sweat rings, and my face has erupted into a blooming case of cystic acne that would embarrass a teenager. My job teaching composition and research has become dull and repetitive, and as the recession decimates public education, people around me are getting furloughed and laid off left and right. My bowels are politely described by my doctor as "really jittery." Most days I plod around feeling like some cosmic force is slowly crushing me beneath its thumb. When I go to Mass, the words to the Apostles' Creed escape me, and I stutter and mumble, silently cursing the tangled, seemingly endless prayer as everyone around me stands erect, at attention, effortlessly letting the words go. When you're supposed to kneel, I stand. When you're supposed to stand, I sit. Mass feels like the world's most complicated game of musical chairs. And I have no idea what to do with the rosary I borrowed from my mother's jewelry box back in high school, when wearing them was somehow rebellious.

But there's some kind of peace I find in church that I rarely feel anywhere else. I sit far back in the pews in a lightless corner, and remain after the evening Mass has ended. The crowd is trickling out, the moon is up somewhere but not visible from here, and I look at the sculpture of Christ, not the suffering, sorrowful Christ I saw in Spanish churches when I was eighteen, not the stained-glass Christ who hovered, glowing, above the altar at my elementary school, but Christ on the verge of being reborn. He's crucified, but his chest is thrust forward as if he were a man saved from drowning, about to begin breathing again. He's alive, again. It's the third day. Mary Magdalene is walking toward the tomb, hands full of balms and soft cloths, totally unprepared for what she's about to confront. "Okay. I'm finally here," I tell him. "This better work."

ONE

The word *catechism* derives from two Greek root words: *kata*, meaning "down," and *echein*, "to sound into the ears." In other words, catechism is indoctrination, and in one medieval illuminated manuscript, the catechism teacher is depicted hollering scriptures through a giant trumpet into a cowering heathen's ear. Today, the church uses Xerox machines to the same effect. A few days before I begin catechism, I go to pick up a folder of readings Father Mellow has left for me at the front desk of the church. It's so thick and bristling with Post-it notes that both hands are required to heft it, and suddenly my suspicions become real: there is a lot of catching up to do.

When I get home and peer into the folder, I find, among other things, an essay by a woman who left her position as a Unitarian minister to become Catholic, a piece about "why Catholics have more fun" (apparently, they dance more at parties, which is news to me), and sheaves of information about how to read the Bible (thankfully, not literally; Vatican II's constitutions encourage Catholics to interpret scripture as something inspired by God rather than swallowing it as fact). There's also an essay by a former punk rocker who says she stopped swearing during her process of conversion. As soon as I read that one, I blurt out, "Fuck that shit," after which I abashedly mutter, "Sorry."

The volume of reading and what it implies about my years out of the church has made me so apprehensive about the first night of class that my already pale face is probably translucent, but I suck it up, put on my glasses to navigate the blue-black evening, and climb the stairs to the meeting room. The fireplace flickers, classical music tinkles out of the stereo, and a few people are chatting. It looks like what I imagined faculty parties would be like before I became a faculty member and discovered that my school didn't have the budget for parties. The class has been on a break for a month and is just coming back together, and as I stand there awkwardly smiling at strangers, I hear snatches of conversations about vacations, kids, jobs. Father Mellow comes over, grabs my hand, and thanks me for coming. He's dressed in street clothes, and I'm grateful; clerical collars still intimidate me. (It's like chatting it up with God's cop when a priest wears one.) At first glance, it appears that everyone here is middle-aged, but soon enough, a couple of young dudes wander in, dressed in sloppy flannels and Vans, and everyone migrates to a loose circle of couches.

There are a lot of people in RCIA, more than twenty. Many people have a sponsor, a practicing Catholic who will guide them through the process of entering or re-entering the church. I don't have one yet. In the case of my class, some of these sponsors come every week, shepherding their charges through every session, and I can't tell who's who. I discover that one woman brings an entire entourage: her husband, her female sponsor, and her sponsor's husband. She tells me it's because they're worried she won't otherwise make it. She was brought up Muslim, married a Catholic in her twenties, and decided after decades of going to Mass that it was time to get baptized; he'd had a couple of heart attacks. One of the class leaders was brought up Jewish, and other students come from various Protestant denominations. Prior to tonight, I had no idea that people were leaving perfectly fine religions for this one. I'd figured only Mormonism made Catholicism look like a logical choice.

A couple of guys are accompanied by their fiancées, young women with concerned eyes who hold the guys' hands tightly for the entire two hours, as if they might otherwise bolt. In order to be married in a church, the guys have go through RCIA or a marriage "immersion program." There's one other youngish woman who appears to be there on her own, like me. I've been coming to weekly Masses for a month to try and prepare and maybe see a familiar face, but I've never seen any of these people before, and I'm painfully awkward around strangers. In a group of potential Catholics who've already been meeting for months, I feel like there's a sign above me reading HEATHEN, and I try to jam my big body more deeply into the sofa so as not to take up too much room.

Things officially begin when Rachel, who's compact, with bright eyes surrounded by a corona of frizzing black hair, announces that they're going to go around the room and talk about a ritual they did at one of the Advent Masses, the four-week liturgical season leading up to Christmas. Fortunately, since I didn't attend any of the Advent Masses, I only have to introduce myself. Listening to the others, I ascertain that one night in December, everyone had to get up on the altar at Mass and talk briefly about why they wanted to be confirmed or baptized Catholic. This sounds like a nightmare. Despite my career as a teacher and the dozens of readings I've given over the course of my writing life, getting up and speaking extemporaneously about faith when you're still in the nascent stages seems terrifying, so I brace myself for a lot of stories of embarrassment and shame and feel terrible for these poor people who had to spill their guts in front of hundreds of strangers.

But this isn't what they talk about. They admit they were nervous, and some of them joke that they couldn't come up with a single reason to be Catholic so they made something up ("I'm just here for the donuts," one guy blurted), but there seems to have been a sort of blessing involved, and people are grateful for that. When the catechumens shuffled up to the altar, their sponsors blessed their heads, shoulders, hands, and feet, and softly made the sign of the cross on each one. You don't see people kneeling down to bless one another's feet all that often in contemporary culture, and the gesture is startling.

When we see an antiquated ritual, rare as sustained eye contact between strangers on a city street, it has the power to shock. Sponsors get nothing for their participation—no heavenly brownie points in the form of an indulgence or time off from making confession—yet most of them come every week, humbling themselves by kneeling down and blessing the feet of their friends, husbands, wives, and children or laying a hand on a shoulder to steady someone.

The circle moves on, and as it turns out, I'm not the only newcomer in the room. There's a rotund, middle-aged guy who says he's coming back to the Church for the first time since childhood, nearly fifty years ago. His glasses are smudged, and he gestures widely, circumscribing circles with the tips of his fingers. He's a historian, and it seems the topic of Catholicism is tough to avoid in his particular branch of history, the history of war. "It's a growth industry," he sighs.

We're given a syllabus for the next few months. Our lessons will be about the sacraments and rituals that go along with them, plus some information about church ministries and an ominous sounding evening on "moral theology," whatever that is. We'll also need to attend certain Masses in order to go through something called the "Scrutinies," which sounds like some sort of torture device the church hauls out of a closet for particularly egregious sinners. Father Mellow quickly interjects that the Scrutinies aren't as scary as they seem; basically, they're a chance for the church community to get to know the catechumens a little and to help purify you before Easter. That's slightly better.

The first sacrament we go over is the logical one: baptism. There's an expression Catholics use for non-converts. They call them "cradle Catholics," and since most baptisms take place when one is a squalling infant, it makes sense. Jacob, Benjamin, Rebecca, and Rachel, the class leaders (or "team," as they prefer to be called, rah rah), each talk briefly about their own baptisms. Jacob, Benjamin, and Rebecca were all baptized as babies and are now well into middle age, so they admit they remember little about the process. Rachel, who converted from a semi-secular version of Judaism, refers to herself as a "baby Catholic," since she was only baptized eight years ago. She describes the weeks leading up to her baptism, when she learned that she wasn't going to have to make confession and felt relieved. "Let's be honest," she says, "I was forty years old and that was going to be a *long* confession." Baptism acts like a kind of blank slate. You get dipped in water, which washes away your sins, and Rachel remembers listening to the *Oh Brother, Where Art Thou?* soundtrack in the weeks before Easter, particularly the song about going down to the water to pray, and feeling a sense of relief; she was beginning again. Two adults in this group will be baptized at Easter. The rest of us will be confirmed, and that means we have to make confession at some point. *Oh shitty shit shit. How am I going to remember all those sins?*

Three years ago, I sort of had a nervous breakdown. I hesitate to call it that, because it wasn't as glamorous as breakdowns seemed to be when I was studying poetry in graduate school. All the breakdown poets seemed to be varnished with at least a little historical gleam, as if their straightjackets were just a bit better-looking than the ones we might someday wear. John Berryman is one of my favorite poets, and his breakdowns were freaking spectacular. When he finally pitched himself off a bridge, he aimed badly and crushed his skull on the riverbank. "Life, friends, is boring," he once wrote. I wasn't nearly that bad, but something was seriously off. Tears were flowing at odd times—while I showered or while walking through the grocery store. Migraines and muscle pain meant that every day I was convinced I had some new disease, Googled it, found out about some other disease, Googled that, and sat sobbing in front of WebMD.com. By the end of the summer I had diagnosed myself with multiple kinds of cancer, arthritis, Crohn's disease, leprosy, Lyme disease, Norwalk virus, lupus, and the plague. This also led to my becoming a paranoid germaphobe, armed at all times with Purell and unable to shake hands with strangers or touch doorknobs without covering my hand with a sleeve. After a billion medical tests revealed nothing but arthritic hands and irritable bowel syndrome, my HMO finally caved and sent me to a psychologist. As soon as she met me, the shrink recommended I come twice a week.

Catholic saints know about depression. Some of them seem to have invented it. Saint Catherine of Siena went so deep into dark trances that she stopped eating, and eventually the only nourishment she took was drinking the infected pus of the sick patients she cared for (disgusting, I know). John of the Cross wrote a book called *Dark Night of the Soul*, and apparently had more than a few of those himself. Even Mother Teresa apparently got down in the dumps quite a lot and punished herself by wearing a spiked band around her thigh, to be tightened when she was tempted to sin. All the mystics had visions, went into trances, and suffered from seizures and mysterious bleeding wounds. Jesus himself cried quite often; you can see him breaking down frequently throughout the gospels, and he wandered off on his own when his ministry got to be too much. Priests and nuns will regale you with stories of people who had breakdowns in seminaries and convents. Going "over the wall" doesn't just mean somebody ran away from their vocation; it also means their vocation freaked them the hell out. Every time I hear one of these stories, I take consolation in knowing that my religion is a bit of a historical loony bin.

Things began to improve slightly with the doubled-up therapy; after all, if you're talking about your problems that often, at least a few of them ought to get resolved. And then after years of dealing with the stress of various relatives dropping dead, my husband Sage and I had a nuclear-scale fight. I'd had my head in books for so long that I'd lost the ability to focus on anything else, and he had been navigating years of mourning. I'd shoved him aside, and he'd burrowed into his sorrows and played music. We lived in the same house on different planets. Maybe artists shouldn't marry; maybe we should just have ridiculous affairs and make art about them and then marry doctors, but like the losers we are, we keep falling in love. The whole mess pointed out something obvious: I wanted to stay married, and I'd been hiding the real state of my marriage under the veneer that I didn't need any help from anyone, ever. Punk rock, gangster rap, and growing up in Oakland taught me to talk tough and act tough, and when people clear the sidewalk as I walk down the street, I know I look tough. But that's just cover for the mushy substance underneath.

My shrink navigated me through all this, and one afternoon she gazed at me in perplexed frustration. "You're angry now. Is there any place you can go where you calm down?" And I responded without thinking: "Church." At that point I was not regularly attending Mass. If anything, I was regularly avoiding it. But some conversations with friends eventually led to my admitting that I missed Catholicism. Most of the left-wing artist types I hung out with thought this was ludicrous. "What, are you going to start listening to Rush Limbaugh?" one of them asked. Another asked—seriously— if that meant I was going to bomb Planned Parenthood. But my friend Eli, who is an atheist Jew, the last person you'd imagine to be okay with religion and Christianity in particular, told me he understood. We've known each other since we were fourteen years old, goofing around at a summer theater camp, and we've been lit-geek running buddies ever since. He was raised in a quasi-Jewish family, but he read

Sartre in college and made up his mind that God did not exist, a belief he's stuck to ever since. When I told Eli that I'd been thinking about going back to the Church, he pulled on his beard and mused, "I'd totally go though the whole Jewish thing, bar mitzvah, you name it. But I don't believe in God." But I do. Oh, that's the trouble. I do.

That's what I told my shrink, and it felt weird to admit it, like blurting out that I believe in leprechauns. Under the tattoos, under the perpetual scowl, under the sheaves of poems and essays I've written beating around that particular burning bush, I have always believed in God, and not the gelatinous New Agey God who keeps cropping up in my "spiritual but not religious" generation's prose, but the biblical God. The Catholic God.

The narrative of a person finding faith in a crisis is a very old one. Even Paul, on the road to Damascus, was in a hot mess. As a persecutor of early Christians who rounded them up for mass slaughter, he knew he was despicable, but it took God putting scales over his eyes to make him understand how bad his behavior was. In the First Epistle to Timothy, he refers to himself as "the worst of sinners." It wasn't much of an exaggeration. Thomas Merton found faith when his parents died. Cast adrift, he partied with writers and knocked up a teenage girl before entering the monastery. Dorothy Day found it as a single mother after the breakup of a common-law marriage, when she was struggling to make enough money to survive and typing up Socialist essays for newspapers.

Today, we turn to shrinks, Prozac, yoga, drinking, television. Crises are supposed to come and go, and we're supposed to deal with them. But when it comes to a crisis because of a desire for faith, none of those solutions seemed to work for me. The contradictory desires for companionship and solitude that pushed me into panic and sorrow mirrored my problem with the phone: I've had a cell phone for years, but fewer than ten people have the number. I want to be able to call out, but I don't want anyone to reach me. And that's what happened to my marriage, after we'd already been together, mostly happily, for nearly a dozen years. I wanted a partner, but I wanted to be alone, to exercise the independence I'd had since childhood. At the same time, my desire for faith meant that I wanted a relationship with God in a community, but I didn't want it to make me into some sort of Bible-thumping right-wing moron. If you're going to admit you're a believer, and you swim in a sea of unbelief, where do you take this overflow of longing, this need?

In my case, you take it to a circle of sofas, in a church, where you're surrounded by seekers who may or may not be facing the same problems as you, but you're all lurching toward Easter like marathon runners stumbling to the tape.

By the second week of catechism, I'm beginning to sort out personalities. There are five young dudes. One of them is

Italian, emotive and over the top; another is Chicano and shy in spite of the massive skull and knife tattooed on his calf; yet another remains silent for the entire time we meet. Two other young guys are roommates: one is small, bearded and quiet; the other is big, clean-shaven, even quieter. The woman who brings her entourage every week is exuberant and funny; her husband has Dante's nose and a graying mustache. The youngish woman who was alone last week is now chatting with a muscular British guy. He frowns a lot, and either he's miserable or it's just the way of his face. The war historian talks and talks, and has that particularly professorial method of circular logic that drove me nuts throughout college and grad school. The guys who are getting married are still here with their fiancées, but it turns out that one of these couples is married already, and the guy has finally decided to convert. His wife still has a death grip on his hand.

We've moved on to the sacrament of confirmation, and Jacob, one of the team leading the class, rubs his thinning hair and explains this usually happens when someone's about twelve. I was in public school that year, so I skipped confirmation. By then my parents didn't really care about my faith: they just wanted me to stop exhibiting bizarre behavior like adopting a block of foam, putting a hat on it, and naming it "Nothing." (Yes, I was a preteen existentialist.) When you're confirmed, you receive the seven gifts of the Holy Spirit: wisdom, understanding, right judgment, courage, knowledge, piety, and awe of God. The Church used to call the final gift "fear of God," which seems much less pleasant. There's so much to be afraid of already that I'd hate to add God to that list. We spend most of the class in small groups, talking about the best gift we ever received, and it's awkward doing icebreakers like this. Group discussions might be something I force my students to do, but they're not something I regularly engage in. The youngish woman and I get to talking. Her name is Theresa, and I can tell we're both treating this experience with a bit of wry distance.

A week later, I get an email from her asking if I'd like to get together for dinner sometime. "I've only heard a little of your story," she writes, "but I think we have things in common." We meet up at a Japanese restaurant, eat a puddle of silken tofu studded with broccoli and mushrooms, and talk about our lives. Theresa is divorced with two kids, in her mid-forties. She works for a large women's rights organization, and I express my relief that nobody's brought up birth control or abortion in our class thus far. "It'll happen," she warns me. "I went to Mass at another church and they talked about the 'holocaust' of dead babies." We both sigh. She grew up in Berkeley in a hippie family that eschewed organized religion, but a void kept nagging at her throughout her life, and she joined the Episcopalian Church to fill it, figuring "they were liberal. You know, like us." But she tells me she never felt welcomed. "The coldest Christians you ever met."

After eating, we set off on a meandering walk through North Berkeley, following the winding streets around the di-vinity school at the top of a steep hill, where we take in the view that sweeps down to the gray sheet of the Bay. Theresa is seriously beautiful; she has shampoo commercial hair and Northern European cheekbones, but she walks slowly, with a shuffling gait. "I'm going in for surgery next week," she tells me as I slow down my stride to match hers. It turns out this is the dozenth surgery she's had in several years. Her second childbirth went awry when a midwife didn't call a doctor soon enough, and her internal organs took a beating. But unexpected things happened when she began exploring Catholicism and started to pray: she began to heal faster than her doctors had expected. "I know it sounds like bullshit," she says, "but after I made confession something really changed." The next surgery will be her final one. After several years of constant pain, she's almost healed.

We start back down the hill. Theresa says she prays a lot these days. RCIA was a logical step for her and a friend who'd been going to Mass together for a while, and her younger son will be baptized at Easter when she gets confirmed. She says that in the worst moments, believing in God came naturally. At some point before one of her surgeries, she imagined Jesus healing her, and she asks me how I see God. I hesitate before answering, "Benign force, maybe?" "And what about the Jesus thing?" she replies. And I'm fucking stumped.

I can't admit this to her, but I've been having issues with Jesus for a while now. Part of it is the way his name gets thrown around in Mass: Jesus lamb of God, Jesus our brother, Jesus has died and risen, Jesus walks on water. Coming from years in the secular world, it feels a little cultish. The only people I ever hear uttering Jesus' name that much are the hordes of evangelicals who set up tables on the central plaza on campus, luring in newly arrived students with cookies and candy, only to convince them they'll burn in Hell if they act on their hormonal impulses or so much as talk with a homosexual. As we walk past North Berkeley's lush Victorians, I tell her that Jesus is kind of a role model, the truest answer I've got.

My inability to answer her question bugs me for weeks, mostly because I'm not sure how I really feel about this Jesus guy. I believe in the historical Christ: there's evidence that he probably existed, but everything written about him came after he died, so no one knows how many miracles attributed to him actually happened. And the virgin birth thing . . . that one's hard. Sometimes I rationalize it, thinking maybe Mary was already pregnant and the Holy Spirit went in and messed with the DNA. But even then, it defies logic: a pregnant teenager is engaged to a much older guy but supposedly never had sex with him, even though the gospels tell us Jesus had brothers and sisters.

Much to Sage's chagrin, I begin filling the TiVo with lots of shows about Jesus from the History Channel and National Geographic Channel, all of which feature awkwardly staged re-enactments probably filmed outside Vegas in the Nevada desert. Sometimes you can see a little neon light in the distance, just like they had in AD 33. The best thing about these shows is that they don't cast some Fabio type as Christ; there's no Hollywood-style wavy, hair-sprayed blond wig and blue eyes. They get Middle Eastern Jewish types to play Jesus, so at least we can picture him as he actually looked: short, skinny, bearded, big nose, brown eyes. The worst part is the acting, which is so wooden that they may as well have cast animated popsicle sticks. The TV shows try to explain how the miracle of the loaves and fishes might have actually occurred (Palestinians were terrible at math), how Christ walked on water (hidden rocks, of course), and how he healed the sick (they weren't really sick, just hysterical, the narrator reveals in his stentorian tone).

I don't find a Jesus I can identify with in the stories about the miracles. They're like novels or old epic poems, just clusters of metaphors, because for someone who's used to finding solace in facts and has taught literature for over a decade, they're tough to believe.

I prefer the stories of Jesus and people, particularly when he's talking to women. When he meets the Samaritan woman at the well, people are shocked he's associating with her, but he just takes her for what she is. She's had five husbands and lives with a guy she's not married to, and she comes from a religious caste Jesus is not even supposed to speak to. He doesn't care. In another story, when the woman caught in adultery is brought to him, he doodles on the ground while waiting for someone without sin to cast the first stone. No one casts a stone, so he just keeps doodling, forgives her, and tells her to go. Women were not treated well in those days, so seeing these women being respected by Christ impresses me. They're certainly being treated better than the Catholic Church treats women today, so it's nice to know that the guy who started it had the right idea.

The idea that forgiveness is waiting for naughty women is something I cling to as Easter approaches, just about six weeks away. One thing festers in my anxiety-riddled mind: Sin. I can almost see it flashing like a neon sign above my head when I sit in church: SINNER. SINNER OVER HERE. TALL BRUNETTE WITH BAD POSTURE. SHE'S A SINNER.

Someone mentioned in catechism that you shouldn't take communion unless you've recently made confession. The last time I made confession was the only time, in elementary school, while I was dressed up as a miniature bride for my first communion and marched onstage for the open confession experiment. At that age, we were taught that everything was sinful. Want a candy bar? Sinful! Mad at your mom? Also sinful! Compared to those venial childhood sins, the shit I got up to in my teens, twenties, and thirties unspools with flashbacks to Sodom and Gomorrah-scale sinning. Even though it's becoming clear that at least a few modern Catholics are pretty forgiving, I still worry the priest hearing confession will not dig my politics.

Speaking with Theresa reassured me that at least one another Catholic in RCIA doesn't toe the line on birth control, but some bishops had recently ordered priests to deny communion to anyone who had voted for pro-choice candidates. The debate over gay marriage rages on in several states, including California, and my gay friends who had recently married were finding themselves in legal limbo. Is fighting for their marriages really a sin? Something tells me Jesus wouldn't think so, but unfortunately, he isn't around to take my confession. He'd probably roll his eyes a little at my histrionics, tell me I'm already forgiven, gay marriage is fine if people love each other, and let me go. But I can't get rid of the idea that I'll be excommunicated before I even manage to step on the altar. So I stop taking communion at Mass lest I choke on the host, and start worrying about the upcoming season of Lent, when "mortification of the flesh"—a terrifying idea, even for someone with arms wreathed in tattoos—is the name of the game. Two words keep pounding in my brain. *Sin. Punishment. Sin. Punishment.*

Each night as I lie in bed desperately trying to fall asleep, every awful thing I've done that day unfurls in front of my eyes. There I am being a jerk to a student. That's me laughing when someone tripped. I'm refusing to give change to a homeless woman with a kid under her arm. And yes, that is me rolling my eyes at some overly loud teenage girls on the train, who responded by calling me a bitch, so I gave them the finger in return. And that's just one day. Before Easter I'll have to try and remember every sin I've ever committed. I ask God for help with that task. And my sleep is always, always troubled.

TWO

Lent begins in late February, and Father Mellow explains to our group that depending on the church calendar, it starts at a different time every year. Easter, unlike Christmas, is a movable feast—a phrase I had previously only associated with Hemingway's memoirs. The Church bases the date of Easter on the Jewish calendar, which means that it usually occurs around the same time as Passover. The Last Supper was a Seder, after all, and Jesus was definitely a Jew. But the exact date of Easter is determined via a nightmarishly complex set of calculations called the "Computus," and damned if I can figure it out. It involves something called an ecclesiastical full moon, the Council of Nicaea in the year 325, a sixth-century Scythian monk nicknamed Dennis the Short, a handful of despotic Roman emperors, and the formula for the Golden Number in the Metonic cycle, which looks like this: $GN = Y \bmod 19 + 1$. I wept in frustration throughout calculus classes in high school, so anything having to do with the maddening calculations of the liturgical calendar goes so far over my head that I give up trying to understand.

I didn't pay much attention to Lent as a child. With the Church trying to soften up its image, we were taught that you just gave up something you liked for forty days. You were supposed to feel spiritually purged as a result, but it was never explained to me how that worked, and when I asked my dad the meaning of "purged," he said it was how you felt after puking. There was no way I was puking for forty days straight. As a kid, I got a minute allowance—just enough loose change to walk up the street to Eddie's Liquors and spend half an hour standing there agonizing over which candy bar to spend it on—so the idea of giving up candy (the suggestion of my catechism teacher) sounded ludicrous. Candy was the only thing I was allowed to buy for myself, and that meant more to me than spiritual cleansing. Whatever I gave up instead escapes me now, but I was left with the impression that Lent pretty much sucked.

RCIA valiantly attempts to reframe this concept to a group of skeptical adults. "When I was a kid," Rebecca, one of our group leaders says, "Lent was about giving up candy and eating fish sticks on Fridays. But today it's more about getting rid of wasteful behavior. Wasted time on the Internet, too much television, that sort of thing. The idea is to think about the time we're wasting and the things we waste so we can get closer to God." This gets my attention, because I do waste a hell of a lot of time on the Internet, and the Internet seems particularly bereft of spiritual benefit. Particularly, I seem to be drawn to the tawdriest, trashiest gossip blogs. My excuse is that it keeps me in touch with the cultural milieu of my students, who seem to do nothing between classes but sit in their dorm rooms torrenting music and movies between sessions of binge drinking and library all-nighters.

But the fact is I'm addicted to gossip. Despite all the time I spend being a pseudo-academic, I still want to say, as Monty Python's Gumbys used to say while bashing themselves on the head with mallets, "Doctor, my brain hurts." My mallet is the life of the mind, a nice place to spend the day, but not where I want to be when I come home. After a ten-hour stint teaching, grading, going to committee meetings, and trying to banter with colleagues much more educationally elite than myself, the last thing I want to do is spend the night reading Hegel or something equally pretentious. Give me a gossipy website and reality TV, thanks.

But Rebecca is right. It's a waste of time, and if I'm going to do Lent right I can give up the gossip blogs for a month or so. Giving up meat on Fridays is not going to be a big deal; I was a vegetarian for over a decade before I got stoned one day, fell off the health wagon, and ate a burger. Why we fast (which in the Catholic tradition means no meat and only one full-size meal) on Fridays in particular, the class leaders don't explain, nor do they tell us why God hates hamburgers, but Rebecca also informs us there's a "no snacks" clause; you aren't supposed to eat anything between your meatless Friday repasts. Hearing that finally tips me back into my childhood annoyance with the restrictions of Lent. Although I work out and don't eat crap, I am nowhere near thin and love to cook and eat.

Voluntary hunger also reminds me of being poor, which I was for much of my childhood and have mostly been as an adult. During lean times in my childhood, we ate food bank groceries, including neon orange hunks of rubbery cheese my father referred to as "Reagan cheese," cheap cuts of meat boiled into submission, produce spotted with brown pits, and anything else that could stretch to feed seven people on a very tight budget. My college and grad school years were all about beans and rice. I have been involuntarily hungry many times, so the idea of willingly going without food is not something I welcome. The rigor of spiritual fasting has a long history in Catholicism; it's supposed to sharpen your senses, thus making you more open to the ways in which the Spirit is sending you messages from God. And, as Rebecca reminds us, it's also a way of being in solidarity with the poor. We're given cardboard boxes from a charity organization, and told to donate to the box the cost of whatever food we're not eating during Lent.

I'm fine with donating. The main issue that bugs me about Lent is the fact that it's all about discipline. You *must* give up meat on Fridays. You *must* go without snacks and eat smaller meals. You *must* give up other luxuries, tithe more of your income, try to volunteer. You *must* act like a good Catholic, a faithful one who is willing to walk with Christ through the bleak days leading to his execution. I've been reading more books by radical Catholics, and it seems for those who take religious vows, the struggles with poverty and chastity pale in comparison to the struggle to follow the third vow: obedience. Clerics must be obedient to their order's superiors, to the Pope, to God. And following orders is more difficult than simply giving up things that please the flesh.

And, in addition giving so much up for Lent, every Catholic is required to go to confession at least once a year, preferably in the week before Easter.

A week into Lent, class meets to go over the sacrament of reconciliation. I don't recognize this term, because it's the result of the Church fine-tuning its language. As it turns out, the term *confession* was scaring people away, because we were all filled with childhood visions of creeping into a dark closet with a pissed-off or bored priest on the other side who sent us home to do endless Our Fathers and Hail Marys. So they did a little Vatican-style rebranding, and the Rite of Reconciliation was born.

Benjamin says he's going to walk us through it by acting it out. He takes a well-worn script in hand, sits face to face with Father Mellow, and begins rattling off his fake sins: porn, alcohol, resenting homeless people and immigrants. Typical Friday night stuff in the average American home. And Father Mellow acts out his part, telling Benjamin (sorry, Benjamin's character) some ways to avoid these things, asking him about maybe going to AA, and sending him on his way with a penance of doing volunteer work with the homeless. "Go now," Father Mellow tells Benjamin, "and sin no more." There's a moment of silence and then somebody raises her hand and says, "Did you forget to tell him to do a few rosaries or something?" Father Mellow laughs and says he always forgets that part, but he can do a rosary if he wants to.

And it seems so easy. If confession had been presented like this when I was a kid, maybe I wouldn't have dreaded it, but it was drilled into us again and again what would happen if you died without making confession (you'd go straight to Hell for complaining about the lunches your mom packed you), plus we heard rumors of priests bursting out of the confessional if a kid said something snarky, grabbing the kid, and frog-marching him or her to the principal's office. Part of the reason I came back to Catholicism was to start over again spiritually, but it seems like the stuff I did in my decades of sinfulness is really none of the Church's business.

Benjamin, Rebecca, and Jacob go on to tell us more about the idea of reconciliation from a layperson's point of view. "It's like being scrubbed clean," says Jacob. Rebecca adds that it's useful for looking ahead at what you want to do with your life. Jacob jokingly complains about how he always has to play the sinner in the re-enactments. And then someone throws them a curve ball and asks, "Exactly what do you mean by sin, anyway?"

Sin is probably the most difficult concept for non-Catholics, and ex-Catholics, to understand. Back in the days of pre-Vatican II Catholicism, most people raised in the Church believed in two kinds of sin: mortal and venial. Mortal sins are the big nasty ones, like killing somebody, cheating on your spouse, and, according to the catechism, being gay and getting an abortion. The latter two are the ones that give me the greatest pause because people are born gay and abortion is a civil issue. The Church disagrees, even though Jesus never says a word in the gospels about either of these acts. The thing that makes a sin mortal is that it has to be a "grave offense," done with the full intention of the sinner; there are no accidental mortal sins. And you can still be forgiven for them by blurting them out in confession, except for abortion, which results in automatic excommunication. By this logic, mass murderers could be forgiven while a terrified twelve-year-old girl raped by a perverted relative would be kicked out of the Church for aborting the resulting pregnancy. I know how ridiculous it sounds. It's what really makes me start to kick over the traces the more I think about the Church's concept of sin, and millions of Catholics, including many of the clergy, feel the same way. But sin has a broader application beyond its most controversial forms, and broken down a bit more, it really becomes a system of checks and balances.

Jesus says in John 5:17 that there is "sin that is not mortal," which the Church defines as less egregious breaches. Venial sins—though the Church doesn't give you a list of them to choose from, and the term has mostly gone out of style since Vatican II—are thus the less offensive, everyday kinds of sins we all commit without really thinking about it. Stuff like not honoring your parents (complaining about all-caps emails from family members), coveting (other writers' book sales, tenure-track jobs), and blaspheming.

Blasphemy is a constant habit that's nearly impossible to break. My automatic exclamation upon stubbing a toe, tripping over a cat, or slamming a car door on my hand is "God-DAMNit!" or "CHRIST!" or "Jesus FUCKING Christ!" I heard streams of this kind of language coming from my father's mouth throughout my childhood and watched him praying in church every Sunday, and there never seemed to be a schism between that kind of language and his stoic, deep faith. I meet lots of Catholics who swear like crazy, including a priest who says "shit" three times in one short conversation and a nun who politely tells me to "stop bitching." Blasphemy really means talking badly about God, and when I say "GodDAMNit," I'm not really addressing that statement to God, but to the broken toe, throbbing thumb, or chipped fingernail polish. Jesus didn't put the cat in front of me to trip over, so when I say "CHRIST!" it's not that different from saying "BANANA" or "TURTLE"; it's just another word.

But Lent is the time of year when you're supposed to work on this kind of thing (on top of everything else), so I develop the habit of apologizing to the ceiling whenever I drop a blasphemy bomb. Jesus doesn't live in the ceiling, but he might be in the sky, or maybe in my hair, so apologies are frequently delivered.

However, there is no way I can get around reconciliation. No matter how many times I deny myself a nice plate of crackers and salami in between lunch and dinner, if I want to make it to confirmation, I have to cough up everything to a priest. Lent starts to bring out my most self-flagellating tendencies. Daily, I mope around thinking about what a slut I used to be, how much of a coveting, jealous, greedy, selfish, perverse, chubby bitch I am. Chubbiness isn't a sin, but right now it feels like the result of sinfulness (snacks), and when I look down at my stomach rolls, I know they're sending me straight to Hell. And that's another concept that causes a lot of confusion for non-Catholics. It's probably Dante's fault that most people think of Hell as a place ruled by a cartoonish devil, like the ones on the cans of chopped ham we ate on childhood camping trips. Most people imagine Satan busily poking agonized sinners in the butt with pitchforks while their feet roast over flames. For English majors, Milton helped create our image of Satan by depicting him as a handsome, muscular guy; in the famous Doré engraving of the Miltonian Lucifer, he's dead sexy, with washboard abs and flowing curls. Temptation personified. We don't ever really get into Hell or Satan in RCIA, but the Internet actually helps me get a better grip on the ideas of sin and Hell, and I don't get it from a gossip blog because I'm not reading those.

Stephen Colbert, as most people know, is a Catholic, and his is probably the only talk show with occasional appearances by a "resident chaplain"—the Jesuit priest James Martin. Some years ago, Colbert had as a guest a professor who'd written a book about Lucifer and our modern concept of Hell. The professor, who had a rather Luciferian goatee, was making a windy argument that Catholics see Hell as the Dante-esque place where you get hot pokers up your bum for all eternity, when Colbert interrupted him and said, "That's not how Catholics see Hell. Catholics think Heaven means being close to God, so Hell means being separated from God." "Oh," replied the professor, obviously annoyed, "you sound like you went to Sunday School." Colbert leaned back and replied, "I teach Sunday School, motherfucker." I watched this clip on YouTube dozens of times before Holy Week. It just makes sense: if sin means doing something that feels like it's offensive to God, as Rebecca tells our class, then Hell means the desolation you feel when you turn your back on God. So sin is really a way of getting people to treat one another better. If you recognize things you're doing that are inherently selfish or cruel, the better your odds are of not continuing to do them. And theoretically, this eventually draws you closer to God.

Colbert's explanation of Hell calls to me in many ways, and not just because he said "motherfucker." While Lent goes on, not only do I start to reframe my thinking about sin as something other than a series of random fuck-ups, but I also start, in tiny, unexpected ways, to grow closer to God. There is no way to talk about this without sounding mushy, but it parallels the way I think about writing. When I was a child, I wrote to impress people. I was so bad at sports that I scored zeroes in every activity at the sports summer camp my parents sent me to, but I could write pretty well, and write reams without a lot of effort. My parents and teachers—all of whom seemed to spend most of their time yelling at me—praised me for it. One teacher told me in fifth grade that I wrote "like a forty-year-old," which seemed great; my parents were past forty at that point, and anything I could do to make me similar to them might result in less yelling. But as I moved on through high school, college, and graduate school, writing was something I did naturally, not something I did to impress people. Sure, I desperately wanted to get published, but I wrote through the bleak years when my manuscripts went out and boomeranged back hundreds of times. I wrote because that's how I made sense of the world, and that's why I write today.

This gradual wading back into Catholicism works in the same way. At first, I wanted Father Mellow to like me, wanted to impress the people in my RCIA class with my cleverness, wanted to obey some of the rules and get them right. But eventually, what superseded my desire to be a textbook "good" Catholic was my growing awareness that God was working quietly in my life. I never experienced a thunderous conversion or literally heard God speaking, and if I had, I would probably have blamed it on my years downing tabs of LSD and mushroom caps.

I begin to find God in lots of unexpected places. God is in the cool water of the swimming pool that surrounds me when I kick off the wall. God is in Bob Dylan lyrics. God is in long conversations with friends, primarily unbelievers. God is definitely in my favorite food: cheese. God is in a good day of teaching; God is in moments when I'm about to start beating up on myself and abruptly decide it's a waste of time. And God is in my husband, who's kept me laughing for more than a decade.

The discipline we put our bodies and minds through during Lent is a pain in the ass, but it does open us up to something else: grace. Living in a state of chronic depression means that one's awareness of goodness in others is muffled. It's hard to appreciate a nice gesture or a kind word when you loathe yourself, and thus you start to take everything that might be good about your life for granted. That's why I keep harping on my sins; somehow, I had gotten the idea that my time away from the Church was about nothing but sinning, and by some people's standards, it probably was. But in order to understand that grace overrides sin, learning that I wasn't a total waste of space or some sort of minion of Satan mattered. I wasn't deliberately hurting people. I love my family even if they drive me nuts. I've never cheated on my spouse, and if we mutually chose long ago not to have kids, to my mind using birth control isn't sinful. But getting to an understanding of that takes a long time.

I worry about how much that choice is perceived by the Church as a sin. In my imagination, as soon as I mention condoms in confession, the priest whips out a cell phone, speed-dials the Vatican, and has my ass kicked out. I tend to hone in on a potential disaster scenario and latch onto it like a pit bull with someone's arm in its jaws. The news carries near-daily stories of the Vatican's hard line on reproductive choice. The fact that I'm freaking out over this at a time when almost every one of my female friends' biological clocks has apparently exploded and I attend eight baby showers in four months doesn't help calm me down. It's great that these women, all feminists, all independently minded, are going to raise independently minded, feminist kids that they really want, but because I'm inexorably drawn back toward a Church that seems to understand women only as mothers or nuns, it's impossible to find a happy medium between my secular and spiritual lives. They're both brimming over with babies.

"I don't think I can go through with confirmation," I tell Father Mellow one night in his office. "The politics . . . I just can't handle it . . . everything they say."

"And 'they' means the Vatican, right?" He's calm as ever and smiles a little, one eye wrinkling nearly closed. "I don't like a lot of what they say either. But Kaya, my spiritual philosophy is *relax*."

I manage a half-defeated snuffle of laughter.

"You've got to understand," he goes on. "There's a big *C* Church and a little *c* church. And the little *c* church is you and me and everyone here. They mean well, but they're not among the people. They get out of touch."

Hearing that helps a little, but I tell Father Mellow I am still pretty sure the increasingly conservative Church sees me as the world's most prodigious sinner, and he simply reminds me of the story of the woman who washes Jesus' feet with her hair, in many ways the New Testament's most shocking anecdote.

One night, Jesus goes to eat dinner at the home of a Pharisee named Simon, who was part of a group of Jewish scribes, and a woman breaks in carrying an alabaster jar of pricey ointment. Out of nowhere, she begins bathing Jesus' feet with the ointment, weeping all the while and drying his feet with her long hair. The first time I read this passage, I found it appalling: it's a sensual gesture, seemingly a total surrender of control. But here's the thing that becomes clearer with a little historical context: she's a prostitute, which we know because they wore their hair very long in those days, and as a result she's the lowest of the low in Judean society. She's weeping because she comes to Jesus knowing she's already forgiven, and unlike the other men around her, he will not use her or judge her for the person she was in the recent past.

Turning toward the woman, he said to Simon, "Do you see this woman? I entered your house; you gave me no water for my feet, but she has bathed my feet with her tears and dried them with her hair. You gave me no kiss, but from the time I came in she has not stopped kissing my feet. You did not anoint my head with oil, but she has anointed my feet with ointment. Therefore, I tell you, her sins, which were many, have been forgiven; hence she has shown great love. But the one to whom little is forgiven, loves little." Then he said to her, "Your sins are forgiven." But those who were at the table with him began to say among themselves, "Who is this who even forgives sins?" And he said to the woman, "Your faith has saved you; go in peace." (Luke 7:44-50)

I had read this story many times, heard it recited by priests and nuns, women and men, gay and straight people. There are many interpretations of it, thousands of commentaries to get lost in. But the bottom line to take from it is this: if you want forgiveness and are willing to ask for it, you're already forgiven. The greatest gift of post-Vatican II Catholicism, in many ways, is the idea that we examine our consciences to decide what we feel is sinful.

In my mind, judging others is a sin I'm definitely guilty of; so are covetousness, selfishness, greed, lethargy, and giving the finger when people don't use their turn signals. Again and again I will take those issues to confession, probably for the rest of my life. But reproductive choice is a different matter: if God didn't want us to use birth control, why did he allow humans to invent it? What about rape victims? If condoms are so evil, why do they save millions of lives? Perhaps the Church would disagree with my line of logic, but my consciousness tells me that Christ would surely forgive me, and I'm not even convinced that he would see my choice as a sin in the first place. Even the moral theologian who was a guest speaker in RCIA was frank enough to say that the Vatican "blew it" when they told women they were not allowed to take the pill in the 1960s. "Men making decisions for women," he declared, "is never a good idea," and I had to hold myself back from leaping out of my chair to give him a standing ovation. No matter which angles I examine it from—and I examine it from many, many angles—birth control never looks like a sin. *The pill sometimes causes an early abortion.*

Father Mellow and I talk for a long time about politics, the big *C* versus the little *c* church, community, books we've been reading, and how he's going to help me find a sponsor for confirmation, because it's a couple of weeks off and I don't have anyone to stand on the altar with me. He never tells me that birth control is okay or anything like that, but he does let me go that evening feeling reassured that I am welcome to join the Church not in spite of the person I am, and not in denial of the way I've lived my life or in denial of my politics or beliefs, but because of who I am, in totality. At that moment, my past might feel like baggage, but maybe hauling that baggage is what got me to return to Catholicism.

Perhaps the austerities of Lent are working their way into my consciousness, because there's a sense of—for lack of a better word—purification as I walk down the stairs and out of the church. My soul is not a blank slate but a chalkboard at the end of a day of many different classes. The writing left behind is faint and layered with erasures and revisions. I can either walk across the hall, run a handful of paper towels under the tap, and wipe it almost totally clean, or keep writing on the dirty surface until nothing I write makes sense. For once in my life, I choose clean.

THREE

THREE

I'm on spring break, with a few days away from my students, who are growing increasingly grouchy and panicked as the semester winds to a close. I'm particularly glad to be getting away from my student Ted, a toweringly tall guy trying to survive a semester of mandatory writing instruction from me. Ted is a textbook nice person, polite and deferential in class, but lately he has been driving me nuts, because every book or film assigned results in an email explaining that "as a Christian, I cannot read books like this/watch this film/have this discussion in class."

Many students at Berkeley belong to one of the many fundamentalist churches that show up on dorm move-in day to help them out before they start asking the students to tithe twenty percent of their scant incomes to pastors who wear Rolodexes and drive Cadillacs and seem to frequently get arrested for sleeping with minors. I hear these kinds of stories over and over from students, many of whom think this is a normal way of being Christian. There's something creepy about many of these groups, but we're a public university with a history of battles over free speech, so the administration tries to ignore the rumors of cultish behavior. At first, I was patient with Ted and explained several times that if he chose a public university, he was going to have to deal with a lot of different subject matter that might make him uncomfortable; he needed to stay open-minded.

But his latest email set me off. Sent the night before spring break, it explains that he can't work on a paper about a film we watched, which included a transsexual character, "because I am a Christian and it made me sick." I start to write back: "Dear Ted: I'm a Christian too, and you need to shut up," but then I close the laptop and walk away. Perhaps I am learning to turn the other cheek.

Sage and I are headed to Gualala, a small town in Mendocino County. He steers the car through the coastal towns, past the lagoon that stretches into a river that later meets the sea, and then we switch places and I take the wheel for the trip up the thousand-foot cliffs that crest over the Pacific. On a road like this, if I'm not steering, I'm going to get carsick. It's a white-knuckle drive even after I've done it several hundred times, including careening down it once years ago, in pitch-black night, with a load of stoned hippies in the back of my truck. Today it's just caffeine that keeps me running, my husband's profile carved out against the window in abstract angles when I glance to the side. Glenn Gould is pounding out Bach through the speakers, hitting the keys so hard it sounds like he's splintering wood. And because Lent is coming to an end, we are talking about the nature of faith. Or I'm talking about it, and Sage is mostly successfully pretending to listen.

We've been together a long time and have always had a theory that part of what holds our relationship together is the fact, on some levels, that we are very different. He's an autodidactic college dropout who taught himself computer programming to make ends meet between gigs; I have a graduate degree but make peanuts for money as a non-tenured lecturer in remedial writing. He plays Cuban music and jazz, sat at his first drum set as a child and fell in love. I flung myself into punk rock, rolled around to hip-hop, wrote my first poems as a small child. He's happy to play in front of any available crowd, whereas I have heart palpitations before every reading I do.

But we both have big noses, impressively big. Our combined nose power would probably cause all the plastic surgeons in L.A. to go into convulsions. We were both born and raised in the Bay Area, two of a very small number among our peer group not to have moved here from somewhere else, and we spy the gentrification around our Oakland neighborhood with a wary eye, tired of watching the place we grew up in slip away. We both grew up broke. We were born in the same hospital, a year and a half apart. We went to high schools three blocks away from one another. His old band played at a club where I tended bar. We circled one another for many years, until we met when he was cooking healthy hippie food in a co-op restaurant around the corner from the bookstore where I sulkily punched the cash register. He came up to the counter with a copy of Plato's *Republic*, and, showing off, I told him I was teaching that book in a college seminar (truth), and that according to Plato, I wouldn't get into the Republic because I wrote poetry (half-truth—Plato wouldn't have wanted me because I'm female). We moved in together a year later.

He doesn't believe in God. This was something I discovered early on in the relationship, and generally, it's okay. I've said before that all my boyfriends over the years were atheists. There was something compelling about their apparently effortless ability to flat-out deny the existence of God. Perhaps, like my desire to nudge many of them into the shower more often, I also hoped I might poke a few holes in their anti-God way of thinking. None of them had really grown up with religion, so it wasn't like their atheism was an act of rebellion. When it came to faith, they had nothing to reject. We are of the generation born to parents who were busy casting off everything they'd inherited—faith, manners, suburban ennui, hygiene—and because I grew up in the epicenter of the Boomers' bratty rebellion, I also grew up among people who never talked about God unless they were seriously high.

At the experimental-learning high school I attended, many of my classmates were from Jewish families, since Berkeley has a rather high percentage of New York-born Jews who came West in the 1960s. But even though those kids had been bat and bar mitzvahed, they just shrugged when I asked them about being Jewish. "My parents go to synagogue like, once a year," a friend told me when I spotted a menorah in her house. If there were any Christians at my school, they sure as hell weren't admitting it. Our teachers tried very hard not to talk about religion, unless they brought up the Crusades in history class and spent several weeks bashing the papacy. I hung my head for that part of the semester.

During my senior year of high school, a group of students went to Spain to study abroad, and my grandparents and parents scraped up enough money for me to go along. As we trooped from medieval churches to baroque cathedrals to museums full of paintings of bleeding, tortured Spanish martyrs and saints, I felt a kind of simultaneous interior pull toward the most haunted-looking art (Goya, El Greco, Picasso's *Guernica*), which appealed to my gloomy teenage mood, and a ton of embarrassment as my classmates—most of whom had never been in a Catholic church before—laughed and pointed at all the depictions of suffering idiots. When we walked through the Prado, glancing back and forth between heavily chinned Hapsburgs with beady, crossed eyes ("Incest!" my teacher helpfully pointed out) and depictions of Teresa of Avila, Spain's favorite loony, brave saint, something made me want to stop and look for a while at Teresa. My classmates, however, were too excited about the possibilities of legal underage drinking to make lingering possible.

Later, we took a train to Avila and spent the day climbing winding stone staircases in abandoned castles. Three of my friends and I escaped the group, bought cardboard boxes of high-potency wine, and spent the frigid afternoon getting drunk on top of the city walls. We didn't visit Teresa's convent, which is one of the city's main attractions, and it was only years later that I read her treatise on mystical relations with God, *The Interior Castle*. At eighteen, sitting on the fortified city walls in my leather jacket, with purple dreadlocks clumping on my shoulders, I couldn't imagine visiting that cold stone city as a pilgrimage. Those walls were built to keep out heathens, and there I was, pretending to be one. Surrounded by the unbelieving children of unbelieving parents in a deeply Catholic country, the only thing I felt about my spiritual heritage was shame.

Every depiction of Catholicism in Spain seemed steeped in that country's heritage of what the writer Federico Garcia Lorca called *duende*—the morbid, mysteriously irrational creative force that permeates Spanish music and art. There was a lot of spilled blood on the church stones we tromped over, a lot of dark, haunted eyes in the faces of Jesus, Mary, and the saints. To my Berkeley-born friends, it was like a horror film: alternately spooky, alienating, and hilarious. But my inner nature is perverse: I loved the sadness of Spanish Catholicism. I wasn't attending Mass at this point, but Catholic guilt crosses all international boundaries, and I would linger by the church doors after my class had filed in on yet another tour, surreptitiously dipping my finger in the Holy Water that always smelled like an old lady's perfume, crossing myself, and then hustling to catch up before anyone caught me in the gesture. Something about the Spanish church made me feel like I belonged, but there was no way for me to articulate it without feeling even more like a pained teenage freak, a way of seeing the world that I unfortunately carried into adulthood.

Lent has the most *duende* of any season in the liturgical year, and my break from teaching comes right at the tail end of it. The days are getting longer; already the hovering purple shadows of winter are being chased off by the arrival of languorous California afternoons, and after years of drought, rain has finally fallen. The pastures of the coastal valleys, dotted with obese milking cows, are vividly green. These rolling hills look a lot like the ones we rode past in Spain, and as I struggle to shake off my dour Lenten aspect, we talk about the landscapes we've been through.

Sage has traveled to play music in Spain several times, and as we drive up Highway 1, our conversation veers from Spain back to Berkeley again. He plays the cajon, the Spanish box drum used with flamenco dancing, and he's familiar with the concept of *duende*; it's often used to describe the raw warbling high notes flamenco demands of its singers. But the idea of *duende* as part of religion is understandably a little hard for him to grasp. His teenage cousin is going though confirmation into the Episcopal Church, and he noticed there was no Jesus on the cross in her church.

"Jesus looked terrible in Spain," he says as the coast unfolds before us. "So Protestants wanted to avoid looking at that?"

"Probably," I reply, "it didn't go with the décor."

"But they have female priests," he says.

"Uh huh," I reply, edging the volume down as Gould hits a particularly manic run on the keyboard.

"What's keeping Catholics from doing that?" he asks.

"Um . . . sexism. Sexism and fear. You know, there were female deacons and priests in the early Church. There are records of that. But then things changed, you know, a lot of fuckery as civilization evolved. It's kinda like the way the U.S. will never have a female president, you know, she might get her period or something . . ." I continue rambling in this vein for a while before I notice he's nodded off.

With Easter around the corner, I've been attending weekday Mass a couple of times a week in addition to Sunday services. The rhythm of Mass, the various gestures and prayers and liturgical patterns, is finally sinking in. I can almost get through the Apostles' Creed without screwing up. Almost. I still stumble on the line "by the power of the Holy Spirit, he was born of the Virgin Mary," which I keep flip-flopping. "By the power of the Virgin Mary, he was born of the . . . oh, crap." Sage is usually out late on Saturday nights playing gigs, and since church means jumping out of bed at eight trying to follow along with a bunch of stuff he doesn't believe in or understand, I get why it's unappealing. But he's interested in what I'm learning, and open-minded enough to talk about it. However, I'm usually in church alone, and often self-conscious about that.

Anyone who attends Mass by herself is guaranteed to be surrounded by what look like hordes of loving Catholic families. There are lots of female lectors at my church, lots of women in the choir, lots of women who attend services, but they're with their families or in groups of other women.

Half an hour after nodding off, Sage wakes up and we meander back to the topic of faith; or, rather, I not-so-subtly steer us back in that direction. While he is intelligent enough to ask lots of questions before making a judgment, a lot of what I talk about from catechism class just doesn't make sense. The idea of confession is particularly confusing to him ("What does the priest do if someone goes in and says they murdered someone?"); transubstantiation, the act of turning bread and wine into flesh and blood, sounds ridiculous when I start trying to break it down ("Cannibalism?"); my moping about Lenten dietary restrictions has made him wary of inquiring any more about that particular ritualistic time period beyond the occasional "When's Easter again?" Even now, on our way up to vacation in a town with maybe four decent restaurants to choose from, the fact that I don't want to get dinner at the barbecue place—which doesn't have any kind of vegetarian options on the menu—is more of an annoyance to him than anything else.

"Tell me why you don't believe in God," I ask him as he stretches his neck. Surprisingly, I've never asked him before. As an adult, I've preferred to leave other people's faith lives alone. When my younger sister married a Jewish guy and they chose to raise their kids in his faith, I just shrugged; if they were happy, fine. When my nieces show up at Easter and Christmas chattering about Passover and Chanukah, I ask them questions, but they're just kids, and their faith formation is different than the one I experienced at their age. Once, my niece picked up my Bible and said, "I've heard of this book." If religion or the lack of it comes up in casual conversation with peers, my usual approach is to change the subject. I don't want people to know I'm Catholic again because it still seems so oppositional to the rest of my life, so I don't bring it up, and I figure I owe them the same right to privacy.

In all our years together, however, I've never pried into why Sage came to the decision to reject religion. But my immersion in RCIA, and hearing stories from former unbelievers who are converting, has made me curious. And after all, I am married to this guy, and although we've grown apart in the last few years, we have been spending more time together, talking and doing things.

"It's not that I deny the possibility of God," he says. "It's just something I don't understand. You know, things around us, where did they come from? Maybe there's something to the idea of having a reverence for nature . . ."

"Fucking hippie," I reply.

"Says you," he replies, shrugging. "Maybe God exists. I just don't know."

"But do you think that there's, like, zero possibility of that, or do you question the existence of God?"

"I think I question it." He pauses and stares out the window. "There's no proof, but who knows?"

"Babe, do you realize what this means? If you don't know, you're not an atheist! Dude, you're an agnostic! Holy shit!"

I'm so overjoyed that I almost roll down the window and shout to the roadside cows, but instead, I switch the CD from Glenn Gould to Neil Young and nod along to the Sasquatch stomp. The thing about realizing my husband doesn't totally deny the existence of God isn't that it means I have a chance of converting him to my own faith. It means that we have gained an inch of spiritual common ground. I don't expect him to embrace the ritualistic side of Catholicism, but if he wonders whether or not there's a God, he might be able to get down with the Mystery.

Right before the consecration, when the priest blesses the bread and wine, he says, "Let us proclaim the mystery of our faith." That mystery is transubstantiation, the admittedly creepy idea that the flesh and blood of Christ appear on the altar. But in a larger sense, there's another capital *M* Mystery about Catholicism that increasingly draws me in. It's the mystery of mysticism, which is as old as Christianity itself. In the Second Epistle of Peter, he writes that by overcoming our physical urges, we might ultimately become "partakers of the divine nature"; in practice, this means we might tap into God via meditation and contemplation. My Buddhist-leaning friends, all part of the "spiritual but not religious" (henceforth: SBNR) arm of my generation, are surprised when I start doing contemplative, centering prayer over the course of RCIA. In their minds, meditation is associated only with Eastern religions, which the SBNRs find a lot less off-putting than Christianity or Judaism, since the floaty yoga pants version of Buddhism many of them practice doesn't have a lot of structure. My brother-in-law, however, a student of the more rigorous branch of Zen Buddhism, totally gets the Catholic contemplative life and is a huge fan of Thomas Merton. What Zen and contemplative Catholicism have in common, something Merton was way ahead of his time in discovering, is that emptying the mind leaves you more open to the divine presence, whether that manifests itself as Jesus, God, the Spirit, or simply as being in a state of Zen. Purification via rituals of meditation or prayer leads to the ability to be more open, and openness leads to our ability to recognize God working in our lives and the lives of others. It is that same pervasive sense of calm I get in conversations with elderly people of deep faith: they have the ability to sit still.

If you live in Northern California and want to find God, you're going to have a lot of luck on the southern Mendocino coast. I'm more of a punk than a hippie, but even I get rapturous when I can see the cliffs slipping down into the Pacific Ocean. My family made regular trips up and down the coast, and the landscapes are as familiar to me as the flat, grimy concrete of Oakland.

We drive into Gualala and pick up the keys to the cabin we're renting, a half mile hike into a protected grove of redwoods. The cabin itself is no great shakes, tiny for two very tall people, with an all-electric kitchen straight out of the 1950s and a kitschy decorative theme of frolicking gnomes. But it's also surrounded on all sides by trees, with a minuscule sliver of ocean visible through the living room windows. It starts raining the night we arrive, and pounds rain on and off the whole time we're there, but neither of us really minds. There're no TV and no Internet, just the piles of books we buy from the bookstore in town, days of relief that I'm now done editing my forthcoming book, conversations, and hikes in between storms.

On Sunday, the third day we're there, at the not-so-horrible hour of 11 AM, we drive into town and find the sole Catholic church at the top of a hill. To my surprise, it's packed, since Gualala is mostly populated by people who fled urban life in the 1960s and 1970s—aging hippies I'd assumed were not drawn to the Church. Mary Star of the Sea is a modern structure with soaring windows behind the altar that offer an expansive view of the redwoods and ocean. Music is provided by a woman with streaming gray hair and her bearded spouse, both strumming guitars. And the priest, an El Greco type with a gray beard, is Irish, and delivers a homily including Katharine Hepburn, the guy who wrote "Amazing Grace" (who turns out to have been a former slave-owner before his conversion), and living in a small community and taking care of each other. "I like this guy," Sage mutters, and I very much like this church. Everyone seems to know one another, and the informality of the setting even extends to the seating— we're on plastic folding chairs instead of pews. The closing hymn is "Amazing Grace." The musician woman tells everyone she had no idea the priest was planning a homily about it, and there's a happy-clappy singalong to that tune before everyone files out, exuberantly hugging and slapping one another on the back outside. When we drive into town after Mass to get breakfast at a café, it suddenly fills up with people from the church, and briefly, as always on these trips, I fantasize about abandoning my academic career and moving up to the town to become a waitress. There seems to be a real community here, unlike back home where I don't even know my neighbor's name. But reality sets in when I remember what a terrible waitress I was.

Upon returning home I receive a gift from Father Mellow: a confirmation sponsor. I was the only orphan in RCIA, arriving without a sponsor week after week, and after I bugged him about it repeatedly, Father Mellow finally tracked down someone with whom he thought I might have things in common.

On Palm Sunday, the week before Easter, Sophia reads the narrator's role in the Passion story. She has a strong presence—her posture is ramrod-straight, her voice is resonant, and she plays out the dramatic pauses and interjections in the long tale of Christ's walk to his crucifixion. I usually attend Mass at a different time than she does, so I've never seen her before. She's in her late fifties and has cropped gray hair and a wry expression, with a complexion tanned by lots of time outdoors. After the service, we go to a café and talk for a while about my gradual drift back toward the Church, the interior battles I have with dogma, and the lefty activism we both participate in. "I'm happy to help you however I can," she tells me, "but I honestly have to wonder why a modern woman would want to be Catholic." She's a cradle Catholic who struggles with most of the same dogmatic and sexist issues I do, but still believes the Church can do some good in spite of its egregious flaws. As we talk, I bring up the issue of gay marriage and how the Church's stance on it drives me nuts. "These friends of mine recently went to Canada to get married," she replies. "They're two women, and I came home to wrap up their gift and found a copy of the local Catholic newspaper with a headline about gay marriage being a moral failing." She shakes her head. "I just set it in the recycling bin and thought, *Well, you're dead wrong*, and prayed for change. Then I mailed the gift."

The thing that helps her cope the most with being a woman in the Church is her prayer group. "I call it pray and bitch," she says. "Pray together, bitch about the shitty parts of the Church." That sounds more than reasonable.

There's something immediately trustworthy about Sophia. Maybe it's her frankness or the fact that she's made a career out of her activism, but mostly it's the fact that she's a woman who finds a way to be Catholic without blindly shuffling along to the rules. When it comes to the idea of examining your conscience, Sophia is a role model. She does Buddhist meditation regularly, and tries to put the Vipassana practice of "loving-kindness" to work in her Catholic life, but she's not afraid to be critical either, and I dig it.

The fact that she also frequently swears doesn't hurt. "The damn bishops really want to humble women with opinions," she tells me. Some years back, the diocese to which our church belongs decided everyone needed to kneel at the consecration, a practice many churches abandoned after Vatican II. In every other diocese I've been to and in the churches I've gone to in Spain and Mexico, people stand during this part of the Mass, so this seems like yet another petty bureaucratic move on the part of our local bishop. But a group of women in our parish decided they were going to keep standing, thank you very much, and I noticed them on Palm Sunday—clusters of proud, mostly gray-haired women, firm-shouldered. "It's a way of saying to the men in charge, 'See me? I'm here,'" says Sophia. At Mass, I'd felt myself starting to kneel, just by rote, and stopped and pushed myself up.

Palm Sunday is the beginning of Holy Week. Triduum, the long weekend of Easter, starts with Holy Thursday, the day of the Last Supper. The RCIA schedule is jam-packed: a walk-through Stations of the Cross and community reconciliation service on Good Friday; a run-through of the confirmation ceremony with our sponsors on Saturday morning; the Easter Vigil on Saturday night; and then Easter Sunday. By the time the weekend is over, I imagine I'll feel as exhausted as if I'd done a triathlon.

Holy Thursday was not a day I acknowledged before I returned to the church, but it quickly turns out to be the most fascinating day in the Triduum for me. At the final

RCIA class, Rachel tells us about the weird ritual we'll be witnessing. "It's called the washing of the feet," she says, and several people, including myself, visibly recoil. "I know!" she laughs. "Nobody wants anyone to touch their stinky feet. But it's very clean, I promise."

In many churches, the foot washing—a re-enactment of Christ's kneeling at the feet of disciples, a towel tied around his waist, bathing their feet in a gesture of humility and service—is perfunctory, with a few men picked from the congregation to represent the apostles. They're usually seated in chairs on the altar, and the priest gives their feet a quick splash before they bolt back to their seats. But at some point in time, probably in the 1970s when the laity were encouraged to play a greater part in the Mass, some churches began to invite a greater participation in the foot washing. So, as Rachel lets us know, anybody in church that night is welcome to have her or his feet washed by a friend, a priest, or a total stranger, and teenagers from the church's youth group will be whisking away the dirty water and towels at regular intervals so that everything remains clean.

That's nice in theory, but I can't even deal with getting a pedicure. If our carefully tended modern feet are still potentially gross, still blighted with athlete's foot and toe fungus, blisters and crusts and ingrown nails, imagine the feet of Christ's disciples, who trekked miles and miles through the deserts of the Middle East in minimalistic sandals and didn't believe in the power of hygiene. That's what makes Jesus performing the act even more revolutionary. He didn't care how nasty the disciples' feet were. He only wanted to express the fact that he was sent here to show compassion.

When I arrive alone at church on Holy Thursday evening, I take a seat in the balcony, where I'm safe from foot washing. Before I left home, I joked with Sage that I was on my way to a mass foot washing, and he cocked an eyebrow, knowing how grossed out I am by feet.

"You're going to touch someone's *feet*?" he asked with a slightly shocked smile. "Would I have to touch someone's feet if I came along?"

"Please feel free to stay home," I laughed.

As I watch the ritual, I'm appalled and absorbed at the same time. Everyone suddenly starts peeling off their socks and shoes, and bowls of water and stacks of towels appear everywhere. In the midst of what looks like watery, podiatric chaos, the first person I spy kneeling to wash someone's feet is a dignified older man with carefully parted white hair, dressed in a beautiful suit, rolling up his sleeves to wash someone's feet. What the hell is going on? It seems like everyone is kneeling and bathing feet, endless variations on pairings of gender and age, a blur of pale toes and arches after the long winter, and it goes on and on for a good half hour. . . . The choir cycles through four or five songs; my back begins to ache in the pew; more towels appear and disappear. If Catholics have some kind of secret foot fetish culture, that's news to me. I spy a pair of people from RCIA, two women who fling their arms around one another once they're done washing, their bare feet slapping on the stone floor as they return to their seats. At the end of the Mass, the decorations in the church are ritually stripped: banners come down, altar cloths are folded, and the hosts in the tabernacle, the vessel where they're stored, are removed from the church.

Father Mellow told our RCIA class that the church does a "living" Stations of the Cross, and I had no idea what he meant until I arrive at church on Friday afternoon. For one thing, it's dead quiet. My church is normally a pretty social scene, with lots of banter in the pews, but on Good Friday it's more like a tomb. Without the decorations, the room looks dark and dull. The fact that it's unusually cold for this time of year adds more funereal ambience to the effect. Father Mellow comes striding in wearing full clericals, a black formal suit with a white collar—he looks smaller than usual—and says the Stations will begin in a few moments. "In the meantime, relax," he says, and a few people out of the hundreds there chuckle. This is not a relaxing atmosphere.

Taped music begins playing, and Father Mellow's miked-up voice announces that we're going to witness the first station. A group of people in street clothes walks in from the back of the church—mostly college students, a couple of older regulars from Sunday service—leading a handsome young guy in a denim shirt. As Father Mellow narrates the fact that this is Jesus' trial, I realize that the handsome guy is supposed to be Jesus, the sweatshirted dudes around him are Roman guards, the older guy in a sweater is Pilate, and the woman in a print skirt is Mary. The Stations are usually just paintings or stained-glass windows, and the most disconcerting thing about this tableaux is the fact that Jesus is so good-looking. Honestly, I never imagined him that way. In order to avoid staring, I try to focus my attention on the wood grain in the pew in front of me. This diversionary tactic works for a few more Stations, as Christ takes up his cross, stumbles, takes it up again, passes the burden momentarily to a stranger, and finally ascends the hill called Golgotha, "the Skull." For some reason, I am shivering in my seat. It's cold, but not that cold, and I realize that we're not sitting here on a Friday afternoon witnessing the re-enactment of someone's natural death. We're witnessing an execution. I lose focus for the rest of the walk-through, as his mother cradles him in her arms, as they drag his body into an offstage tomb. Silently, I offer up a little prayer to God: *Please forgive me for noticing how cute your son is, sorrysorrysorrysorrysorrythanks.*

Confession comes an hour or so later whether I want it to or not, after waiting in a very long line with all the other once-a-year sinners who'd like to be purged. There are four or five priests scattered around the inside of the church, each of them tucked back into a corner, with a line of people spiraling out from each priest into the body of the church. I find Father Mellow in one corner close to the altar, and his line is the longest of all. It stretches all the way to the back of the church, past the pews where latecomers sit during Mass, past the rickety wooden table where the bread and wine usually sit waiting on Sundays, back into the shadowy narthex. I'm at the very end of the line. The guy in front of me moves a rosary through his fingers behind his back—*clack, pause pause, clack, pause, clack clack pause*—and the hypnotic repetition seems to make the line move more slowly. Squinting in the dimness, I see Sophia across the room, a few people from RCIA, faces from Sundays. Everyone looks downcast and grim. I shuffle a few inches forward to the rosary's *clacks*. Once people finish confessing, they practically sprint from the church, and I start counting the seconds it takes each of them to get to the heavy front doors.

Resisting the urge to bolt, I try to reduce my anxiety by squeezing my hands into fists, but as a result my palms get sweaty, and I have to frequently wipe them on my jeans. Although people are trying to whisper their confessions, some are more successful than others; little words of sin float up into the air around us. Anger, drinking, unhappiness, resentment, hate. I spot a guy across the church checking his cell phone and remember that there's actually a confession app for iPhones, which might have proved helpful if I owned one. Instead, I'm going to have to rely on my memory, which is so full of fissures and willful revision that God will probably just have to deal with whatever comes out of my mouth.

When my turn comes, Father Mellow gives me a reassuring smile and cheerfully says, "Hi, how are you?" as if we just happened to cross paths. I clear my throat, erroneously skipping right over the part we were instructed on in RCIA, where you're supposed to say, "Forgive me, father, for

I have sinned." "Okay, I've done some stuff," I begin, always eloquent under pressure. And maybe because I've had so much experience with shrinks, or because I'm jittery, or because Father Mellow makes it easy, confession is over before I know it. "Go now," he says with a smile, "and sin no more." I almost burst into inane laughter, the release of pressure is so unexpected and welcome. It's as if I've been walking around with blisters on my feet for decades, and suddenly remembered that it only takes a pinprick to get rid of them. Once I pass through the doors when I'm done, I don't look back.

It's Saturday, the day of my confirmation, and I'm still trying to decide which saint to adopt. Catholicism is the only branch of Christianity that believes in the intercession of the saints. Basically, if you have a specific need, you pick a saint who's the patron of whatever it is you're asking for, and ask him or her to go bug God on your behalf. Since they're already in Heaven, it's faster for them to get to God; they can just amble on over.

There are many saints with utterly bizarre lines of patronage. Saint Clare of Assisi, who has become one of my favorite saints, is the patron saint of television, which would probably surprise her because she died in the thirteenth century. The Irish saint Fiacre is the patron saint of venereal disease, mostly because he was so averse to being around women (logically, the Vatican should have chosen a Lothario for this job). There are patron saints for bald people, chicken farmers, button makers, juvenile delinquents, sellers of second-hand clothing, and almost any other occupation or lifestyle you can think of.

Catholic kids pick a saint for confirmation based on whatever they identify with about that person's life, or what that person represents. Oftentimes, people get lazy and just pick the saint with their name. My middle name is Joan, so Joan of Arc seemed like a logical choice at first. I'm actually named after Joan Baez, who is not a personal friend of the family or anything like that; my dad just had the hots for her, and I think my parents were running out of ideas for girl's names by the time I was born. (Every time I hear "Diamonds and Rust," I get a little embarrassed thinking of my father mooning over the record player.) But when I started researching Joan of Arc, I wasn't sure she represented the kind of Catholic I wanted to be. I loathe violence, don't have visions, and can't ride a horse, and it's hard to find armor to fit over my chest. Joan is a great saint, especially if you are French or a soldier, because she's your patron, but if you're a pacifist writer, she doesn't quite fit the bill.

Most of Saturday morning is spent digging up information about female saints. I was baptized as Catherine (and why I changed my name is a story for another time), and there are several Saint Catherines. Saint Catherine of Siena is the best known, as she was one of the great mystics, a political agitator, a woman so enraptured by God that she stopped eating and drinking until she died. She could levitate herself, thus becoming part of a short list of flying saints that includes one of my favorite saints who probably never existed, Christina the Astonishing, who's cool enough to be referenced in a Nick Cave song. This is all well and good, but Catherine of Siena is the patron saint of firefighters, nurses, and the Theta Phi Alpha sorority, and I don't fit into any of those categories. The other Saint Catherines—of Alexandria, of Bologna, of Sweden—don't really do it for me either. One was tortured to death on a wheel; another's corpse is still preserved in full view (these saints are charmingly called "the incorruptibles," which sounds like the name of a punk band); another had a deer come and chase off some young toughs trying to rape her. Good stories, sure, but nothing that gets at the quest I'm on.

As usual in times of distress, I start Googling. My search string "patron saint of sinners" turns up a few gothy MySpace band pages. And it also turns up Mary Magdalene.

Much of what we know about Mary Magdalene is crap. There's no evidence she was a prostitute, because that comes from early biblical scholars who mistakenly conflated her with the woman who washes Jesus' feet with her tears. Dan Brown would like us to believe she married Jesus, bore his child, and launched a lot of best-selling trashy novels, but even though that may be based on some rough historical evidence, it's pretty much crap too. People who saw Scorsese's *The Last Temptation of Christ* like to picture her as a sexy Barbara Hershey, covered in tattoos and writhing around. But that doesn't reveal much about her either. All we know, even from the Gnostic gospel that bears her name, is that Mary Magdalene was an apostle to Christ, who drove seven demons from her, which may have actually been illnesses of some sort; that she and the four or five other female apostles stood at the foot of the cross after the male apostles punked out and went home; and that she was the first witness to the resurrection. There are some wonderful apocryphal stories about Mary Magdalene: she rode in a stone boat to France and meditated silently for thirty-three years; she was a visionary and leader of the early Church.

We may not know a lot of facts about her, but it's clear from the evidence that she was a woman of her own means. She chose to follow Jesus as an adult, and thus she made that choice as a fully formed person. She's the patron saint of contemplatives, penitents, sinners—all forms of women who go looking for ways to change their lives.

On Saturday afternoon, when I hand Sophia the card with Mary Magdalene's name written on it so she can flash it at Father Mellow during the Easter Vigil, she smiles. "I always think of her as the first female priest," she says. Maybe that's what draws me to Mary Magdalene, the fact that she got there so early. Mostly, however, I admire the fact that she got there on her own.

At the Easter Vigil that night, Father Borough moves through the darkness of the church lofting the three-foot-tall Paschal candle, specially made for this once-a-year ritual. His thick New York accent makes the two-thousand-year-old incantation of *Lumen Christi*—"Christ Our Light"—sound like something James Cagney might have intoned in the role of a scrappy altar boy. The entire church is pitched into darkness, the pews packed. It's impossible to achieve a collective hush among hundreds of people. Everywhere there are poorly muffled whispers and belching cell phones. A sacristan—the woman who handles the sacred objects like the chalice and vestments—swings a thurible, which looks like a smoking kitchen colander. Father Mellow and Father Smiley trail along, dressed in white robes, and by the time they all hit the altar with only a few stumbles in the darkness, the church is acrid with resinous-smelling liturgical smoke. Father Borough pulls a lighter out of his robes, sets fire to some kindling in a big metal bowl, and lights the Paschal candle from that, and it is passed from one parishioner to another. "The light," he says, looking us over, "has come into the world."

Sitting, for once, in a front-row pew where all the catechumens have been herded, I lean over to Sophia and whisper, "This is *great* theater."

I don't mean to dismiss the Easter Vigil as an exercise in style. It is the most important holiday on the Church calendar, when people renew their baptismal vows, catechumens and candidates are received into the Church, and we celebrate the most insane belief of all: that three days after being crucified, Jesus got up and walked out of his own tomb. But with its extravagance of Bible readings; its only-sung-once-a-year prayers of the Exsultet and the Litany of the Saints; its grandiose music, the whole three-hour ritual witnessed by a congregation that actually dresses up instead of arriving in its usual Northern California schlub attire, Easter is pretty fucking impressive. It's almost as if the church, so constrained for the rest of the year, finally decides to pull out all the stops, in a "How do you like me now?" kind of move.

Sitting with my RCIA group, I want to resist this spectacle, but something about its antiquated nature is haunting, as if the entire congregation has been beamed back thousands of years. The Exsultet, sung a cappella by a trio of cantors, is like nothing I've ever heard before: a kind of medieval call-and-response, with an incantation of Christ as "the morning star who shed his peaceful light on all mankind" (which sounds less New Age goopy in Latin: *Christus Filius tuus, vivit et regnant in saecula saeculorum*). It's like something the women who greeted Christ upon his resurrection might have sung outside the tomb.

Eventually, the two people being baptized are called up to the altar. One of them is the gregarious, chatty woman who brings the huge posse each week, and the other is Theresa's six-year-old son. They have to lie prostrate on the altar throughout the incantation of the Litany of the Saints, which goes on and on, and the six-year-old, with his mom kneeling and holding his hand, lies right down with a thud. The sheer weirdness of seeing someone lying face down in public without being drunk is jarring enough until I realize that they must really want to do this if they're willing to put their faces on the dirty stone. (In the six-year-old's case, I recognize that he's just being a good kid, but I can't imagine my own six-year-old niece lying still for anything.) As we all chant along, incanting the names of the ancient saints, the martyrs, the Desert Fathers, and all the makers of the early church—Agatha, Lucy, Agnes, Ambrose, Damian, Bartholomew, and so many others—I silently add my own names to the list: Harvey Milk; my colleague recently gone from breast cancer; my friend Tom, dead from AIDS years ago; and my grandparents, mother-in-law, dad. Catholics often pray to God through the intercession of the saints, and I figure I need as many of them on my side as possible, so I add the names of people I love who have died. If one of my saints was a Radical Faerie who walked around handing out AIDS testing brochures while wearing sparkly wings and a kilt and holding a joint in one hand, all the better.

During the baptisms, the little boy goes first and is plunged into a tin bathtub that looks rather like a horse trough. Later, Theresa tells me volunteers spent an hour ferrying buckets of hot water down the stairs to fill the tub so it wouldn't be cold by the time of the Vigil. The adult woman follows him, and both are whisked drippingly away to change into dry clothes. Afterward, Father Borough asks us to collectively renew our baptismal vows. ("Do you reject Satan and all his works?" "Well, why not?" I say in my head) He then takes up something that looks like a horsetail and a bowl of Holy Water and goes up and down the aisles, sprinkling the congregation. I glance back to see my husband, seated a row behind my group, getting smacked right in the face with a brushful of Holy Water. He wipes it away, and I catch his eye and mouth, "Sorry about that." He smiles back, patiently. This is a very long haul for an unbeliever.

When Father Mellow invites the people being confirmed to come up to the altar, I start to get nervous. If God's going to smite me down, now would be a good time for it to happen, because I'm highly visible. Sophia stands behind me. We're asked if we sincerely want to be Catholic, at which point Father Mellow whispers, "Say, 'I do,'" which we do. As he moves down the line, he says aloud each saint's name, all uncannily well chosen. There are two doubting Thomases for the loud guys and a couple of obscure female saints for the women who rarely spoke, and the guy next to me confuses me for a minute by choosing a saint named Ivo, which sounds like Emo to me—not a long shot, given his haircut. Father Mellow smears our foreheads and cheeks with chrism (blessed oil mixed with a lot of cloying, resinous perfume) and whispers, "Receive the Holy Spirit."

"Mary Magdalene," Father Mellow calls me, and the chrism drips off my face. Sophia rubs my back. Emo mumbles, "This stuff is burning!" and suddenly I realize that my forehead is burning and itching like crazy too, and I start giggling semihysterically and the congregation applauds and I'm back in the pew, dabbing my oily forehead with a Kleenex. I haven't been struck down, and through this sacrament, I'm now in full communion with the Catholic Church, whether it wants me or not.

❈

I wake up early on Easter morning, waiting to see if I feel any different. Not really—just worn out and raggedy. The Easter Vigil fulfilled my church-going obligations for the weekend, so I don't have to go back again. Sage is still asleep and I need to get out of the house, so I grab a DVD that needs to be returned and get into my car, steering through the flats and over the hills toward Piedmont Avenue. It's dead quiet out; everyone must be sleeping in. After I stuff the disc into the store's slotted door and get back in the car, instead of turning left onto Pleasant Valley Road to head home, I drive without thinking straight across the intersection and into the massive cemetery.

I haven't been here in years. It's full of showy monuments that belong to wealthy California families. Lots of locally famous people are buried here: Julia Morgan, Bernard Maybeck, the Black Dahlia, Mac Dre. There's a large area of early Chinese graves from the first immigrants to the area as well as a Jewish section, and over on one of the sloping sides, many of the poor Irish families who populated West Oakland before it became a largely African American neighborhood during World War II are clustered together, crammed in as tightly in death as they were in life. Among these crowded graves are my paternal grandparents, my father, his extended family, and his brother, who died as an infant. I used to come here a lot as a teenager to drink and walk around; after my dad was buried here, this was no longer an attractive activity. It's been over a decade since I drove through these gates.

The guardhouse is closed, so there's nobody inside with a map to show me where my family plot is located, and damned if I can remember. As I'm driving in circles, wondering what the hell I'm doing here and if I should just turn around and go home, a big scraper car pounding out rattling bass beats starts tailgating me. I've lived in Oakland my whole life, and I know I just need to get out of the way—this dude is going to tailgate anywhere he drives, even in a cemetery, but there's no place to pull over on the narrow roads. The car goes *BAMP . . . BAMP . . . BAMP . . .* bass shaking my plasticky econo model, and panic starts creeping up the back of my neck. I'm not afraid of the guys in the car; I'm panicking because I'm increasingly lost: the lanes of graves keep unfolding and unfolding, one hill flattening out to more graves, another one crested by a mausoleum. Finally, there's a turnout, and I pull into it as the *BAMP . . . BAMP* starts to fade out when the dudes peel away.

Out of the car and trying to catch a deep breath, I look down at the flat stone under my feet and read the inscription. And now I can't breathe, and more scraper cars whiz by the weeping white lady in front of her father's grave. "Oh Dad," I say. "What the fuck? How the fuck did this happen? What the fuck, what the fuck, what the fuck . . ." He's been with me a lot lately, his hunched praying shoulders always hovering in front of me when I'm in church, his drinking and premature death padding after me in my anxieties and my sorrows. Sometimes I wondered if I was only back in church because I never made peace with his absence, as if I were chasing a particularly ornery ghost through the dark caverns of Lent, only to find myself here, on Easter morning, something guiding me along.

One thing is clear: if God brought me back to my father, it's because I need to move on. And that's what I say to him, over the thundering bass of the cars clustering around a freshly dug plot up the hill, evidence of another wasted young life in Oakland's never-ending war with itself. I need to let go of my regret over losing my father not because he had me baptized, not because I sat beside him in church and he foisted a love of this ridiculous religion on me, not because he loved me even though he never said it aloud, but because the past is heavy baggage, and my father's death is part of the past. It's been nearly twenty years. In all these days of Lent, of the Triduum, in this Easter morning moment, God has been reminding me that I am no longer a wounded nineteen-year-old. The funeral is over. Now is the time to be new.

FOUR

The day after Easter, Sage and I get dressed up in nice outfits and meet up with our friends Seraphina and John for dinner. Clomping around like a tree trunk in heels and self-consciously gazing around at the more casually dressed diners in what passes for a nice restaurant in Berkeley, I feel more than a little out of place. "It's like we're going to an adult prom," Seraphina observes. She's right. With Sage and John in natty suits and fedoras and Seraphina and me in dresses, we look like bespectacled and tattooed kids twenty years late for our adolescence. We're styling ourselves in honor of Leonard Cohen, who's touring for the first time in more than twenty years. The last time I saw him perform, I was in junior high, and watched bewildered as identical blonde twin girls in sailor suits tried to rush the stage at the end of the show. Cohen was halfway gone by the time they arrived, but he marched right back toward them, smiling like a wolf and cocking his hat back on his head.

Exhausted and emotionally wrung out, I'm probably not in the right frame of mind for hero worship, but we bought these tickets months ago. Even though I have slept maybe eight hours in the last three days, the Paramount Theatre—a gilded Art Deco wonder, one of Oakland's only braggable landmarks—awaits. We walk by the idling tour buses, where dozens of guys in suits and fedoras mill around. Even the stage crew is impeccably dressed. The show starts on time, no opening act necessary, and the seventy-five-year-old singer bounds onto the stage, whisking the microphone along with him, and proceeds to play for four fucking hours.

It's almost punishing. I keep fidgeting in my seat through the boring B-sides I don't like, closing my eyes through the songs I've sung since I was a child. Cohen's music was obsessively played in my home until every one of my siblings and I could sing along to most of his tunes, like the world's saddest kinder choir. Cohen is the closest thing to a religious figure pop music has to offer: he's a Zen monk and a Jew, and Catholic imagery threads through his lyrics. Knowing I have to get up at 6 AM tomorrow and go teach for ten hours, I become increasingly petulant and wriggly until things finally wind down. When the end finally comes, Cohen blesses the audience, his gravel pit voice intoning a prayer for all of us: "May you be surrounded by friends and family. And if that is not your lot, may the blessings find you in your solitude." After my adventure in the cemetery yesterday, I can't manage a tear, but in my mind I tell Cohen I would offer one up if I could. Saints are everywhere, even in Oakland.

My book is due to arrive any day. But my editor quits two weeks before the book's release, leaving me in the hands of another editor who is subsequently laid off. In the course of two weeks, I cycle through three different publicists, each of whom leaves the corporation without telling me. And so the book's release is not greeted with a feeling of accomplishment, but with a low-grade, pervasive panic that hums like an engine of doom.

In this cloudy atmosphere, I also have to go on a book tour. And this too is suffused with a sense of doom from the get-go. Planes are late. It's raining in several cities, and traffic is snarled and disastrous. My stomach churns before and after every event. Three people show up at one reading and five at another, and I know from working in bookstores that those are not exactly blockbuster turnouts.

But throughout this trip, I keep looking for a way to keep a line open to God. It's hard when I walk into a room full of empty chairs, or call the publisher in New York only to discover someone else has been laid off. When the world's kicking your ass, God sometimes seems to back off. So instead of telegraphing desperate prayers to the Man, I start sending messages via my patron saint Mary Magdalene: *Hey Mary, could you please tell God I need it not to be raining in June while I'm wheeling a suitcase around Seattle? Hey Mary, can you help me make this train to Portland? Hey Mary, could people maybe buy at least five fucking books?* And because she's a woman who dealt with a lot of shit and sorrow, Mary Magdalene delivers. My older sister lives in Portland and works the phone lines to rustle up a good twenty people to plug the crowd. I manage to sell a decent number of books and befriend the events guy at the bookstore, another writer scraping together a living. Thank God for Oregon, and especially for its oppressive weather, which forces people to read.

My sister is almost a decade older and left for college while I was still pretty young, so we grew up at a physical distance. She's been in Oregon for decades now, flying home a few times a year to visit, but otherwise up to her elbows in viscera and horses. To clarify, she's a doctor who raises horses, not a horse doctor, though I'm sure she'd be good at that too. Superficially, we don't have much in common; she's outdoorsy to my dimly-lit-room kind of literary lifestyle. But we slide right into being around one another like no time has passed, even if these trips are the only time we really hang out. Her husband of many years is an on-and-off student of Zen, and a few years back, he'd actually dragged the whole family all the way to Japan so he could go on a long sit and discern whether or not he wanted to become a monk. I find a photo of the family on a shelf—him, my sister, and his kids from a previous marriage—all dressed in blue kimonos and gathered around the round-faced, bucolic roshi. I wonder why

Buddhist priests always look jolly. Zen is tough stuff, the most disciplined and strenuous form of Buddhism.

My sister tried a few silent retreats to get a sense of what her husband was doing but was too restless to make it work. I ask her if she'd ever go back to the Church, and she says no. "If there was a parish like yours up here, maybe. I just got too much of it as a kid." During her K-12 years, she went to Catholic schools often run by strict, humorless nuns. That's probably enough to snuff faith out in most people, let alone my sister, who likes a good laugh and needs one after a day in the operating room. But it bothers me that out of the five kids in my family, I am the only one who pursued Catholicism into adulthood. I think my brother attends Mass on occasion, but none of my three sisters have anything to do with it. It doesn't seem to be a failing on the part of our parents; rather, it seems more like we were given too many options as adults, none of which squared with the way we saw the Church as kids: a kind of monolithic object that our dad bent down to when he dragged his hangovers and sins before it.

The book tour leaves me frazzled, and upon returning home, I'm still wrestling with how damn lonely being Catholic feels. Sophia goes to Mass at a different time than I do, so we don't share a pew. It's been four weeks and I haven't seen the RCIA group since we met one last time for a potluck and talked about our experiences of Easter while eating fried chicken and brownies. Where they went—to another parish, out of town, away from the church—I don't know, but when I look around for them at Mass, there is no one to be found. Then, I find myself sitting next to one of the couples. When it comes time to shake hands and offer one another peace, they offer zero sign of recognition. Nobody other than Father Mellow seems to give a damn that I'm at church. Every Sunday as the crowds surge by to greet him after Mass, we play catch-up for a few moments.

There has to be a regular way to hash out these issues with someone, and Mary Magdalene must have really slapped God around on my behalf, because an email from one of the RCIA leaders informs me that the local theology school is offering an "at-home retreat": twice-a-week meetings with someone called a "spiritual director" for most of July. "Oh, why not," I mutter, sending an email to the guy who runs the operation. At worst, I figure I can learn more about the theoretical questions that keep bugging me after Easter: transubstantiation, Heaven, Hell, the virgin birth . . . the kind of stuff that every Catholic kid learns but I somehow skipped over.

The theology school is broken up into multiple schools, each focusing on a different kind of Christian belief, along with an Islamic institute, a Buddhist school, and a center for Jewish studies. There are three Catholic schools, each training seminarians and a few laypeople; one is Franciscan, the other is Dominican, and the one I'm going to participate in is Jesuit.

I don't know much about the Jesuits other than the fact that they run a university in San Francisco where I once applied for a job. Jesuits don't have a distinctive garb like Trappists or Franciscans, so you wouldn't be able to tell a Jesuit from an average guy via his wardrobe if one of them wound up in a lineup. So I go into my first meeting completely ignorant of Jesuit thought, Jesuit history, and Jesuit spirituality, which I soon learn is a radical school of its own.

I meet him at a building at the top of a steep hill. A small trickle of men, all of them clean-cut and casually dressed for Berkeley summer, flows in and out of the doors as I stand there waiting, and soon enough, one of them walks up to me and says, "Kaya?" magically pronouncing it right. He ushers me into a side room and closes the door behind us. Italian, maybe in his mid-thirties, he has blond hair, big blue eyes, and round cheeks that seem to constantly flush red. This combination makes me think of the face of a cherub depicted in a fresco. Italians have a way of making you romanticize them, intentionally or not. He's wearing a shirt with the Jesuit logo—a sunburst around the letters IHS, an ancient monogram for the first three letters of Jesus' Greek name, *iota eta sigma*—stitched onto a pocket. Jeans, sneakers. He could be any grad student whom I grouchily bump into while waiting in line for my morning coffee. We begin introductions, and I ask if he's a student at the school. "No," he replies. "Already I am ordained. I am a priest." And in response, I say, "Cool." I have never been around a young priest before.

Aside from being young, this Italian priest is really different from the priests I know. For one thing, he has a way of leaning his chin onto his hands when I'm talking, and he blushes the whole time, shyly gazing toward the floor for long pauses when I bring up some particularly tricky theological point. For another, I'm different than the people he's used to talking to; he's familiar with the idea of RCIA, but in Italy, he tells me, "everybody is Catholic already. Nobody comes into it as an adult." And he admittedly struggles with English, taking a while to find the right word, which is often wrong, and stringing things together in a manner I'm not going to reproduce, because it would make him sound like a spaghetti-twirling character from a bad film, when in fact he's highly intelligent and very well read.

Much of our first conversation is understandably heavy on the pauses and questions and repetitions. I mumble some things about being adrift in my faith life, not being sure why I'm Catholic, and Mary Magdalene, and he nods and asks me to repeat a few things and, suddenly, an hour is up. "I'll give you some reading," he says, and sends me home to read a couple of gospel passages: Mary Magdalene at the tomb, in the Gospel of John, and the woman who washes Jesus' feet with her hair, in Luke. Again. At this point I could complain that men keep making me read that passage because they think I'm some sort of reformed prostitute, but I know that's not the case. When a woman comes to them asking for answers, talking about what a shitty, sinful mess she used to be, it's a story that offers some consolation.

A good student, I go home, do the reading, and return two days later. "And what did you feel when you read these?" he asks. And I explode into a torrent of slobbery tears. This is mortifying: I never cried in front of Father Mellow, never shed a tear in church. It takes a really, really bad day to make me cry even in therapy, and yet here I am, bawling in front of a near-stranger who simply asked me a question about some two-thousand-year-old texts.

"I'm sorry," I say, snuffling into the proffered tissue. "I never cry, seriously."

"It's okay," he replies. "I'm a priest; I'm used to it."

And that makes me laugh, and we begin talking about what it was that snapped the bawling switch over to "on."

In the passage from John, Mary Magdalene goes alone to the tomb of Christ in order to anoint the body; back in the days before refrigeration and formaldehyde, this was a necessarily gruesome task because bodies rapidly began to rot in the Middle Eastern heat. Of course, she gets to the tomb and discovers the boulder rolled away and no Jesus inside, at which point she understandably freaks out and begins sobbing. Jesus, who's kind of sneaky in John's telling, walks up to her and asks why she's crying. She doesn't recognize him—John says she thinks he's a gardener—and she replies, "They've taken my Lord away, and I don't know where to find him." The Italian stops me here—I have a bad habit of rehashing everything I've read to people who probably know this stuff by heart—and says, "So how does Mary know it's Jesus?"

"Well, he talks to her."

"Yes," he says patiently, "but what does he say?"

"Something about not being the gardener?"

The Italian catches my eye and leans forward. "He says her *name.*"

"Oh, right . . ."

"So," he continues, attempting a small smile, "do you think Jesus ever says your name?"

And I start wailing again. It's quite embarrassing, and he again has to wait for me to wind down. The truth is that if Jesus had ever said my name, I would run fast as hell to my shrink and ask to be put in the bin. Visions and voices are not my thing. But the Italian explains it's more about being open to God; Jesus is God in human form, and the first thing Mary Magdalene does when she realizes it's Jesus is to try and embrace him, a very human impulse. So our job is to be open to finding God in other people, in the most unexpected circumstances. Of course, when she goes to tell the apostles what's happened, they don't believe her. "Typical men," I mutter. And it's time to go.

Spiritual direction has a long history in the church, although until fairly recently, it was usually reserved for people in holy orders. Vocations are tough, and while there's no exact number available since many people simply walk away when they no longer want to be in orders, the rate of attrition from the priesthood, monasteries, and convents is roughly half the rate of applicants. The Church long relied on older priests and nuns to assist novices in their training, and those conversations formed the model for the kind of spiritual direction I'm doing with the Italian.

Of course, laypeople have long sought out religious advisors in times of crisis, but in the secular world I dog-paddle in, we go to therapy. It helps if one has insurance. In recent decades, the Church has been hemorrhaging followers, and faith crises are a dime a dozen. So the Church began training priests and nuns to counsel laypeople in the hope of keeping them. The Jesuits were at the forefront of this, and now they even train laypeople to be spiritual directors. I'm used to therapy; I know the lobby in my shrink's office, with its arty prints, old issues of *Sunset* magazine, and kilim rugs, better than my own office at work, but the notion of talking with her about God doesn't quite work. She knows a lot about the mind, but I'm not sure she's an expert on the soul. And my soul is clearly in need of counsel.

Thus begins the era I refer to as "crying in church." That Sunday, Father Mellow announces that the priests will be doing the Sacrament of the Sick for anyone who needs it. This used to be called "extreme unction"—a Catholic phrase if I've ever heard one—and was reserved for people on their deathbeds. You've probably seen it depicted in films, the priest flying into the hospital room with a bottle of Holy Water to do some mumbo jumbo over a bitter but suddenly penitent old dude who realizes his whole life's been a waste. But these days, the Church sees it more as a kind of spiritual health insurance. If you're going in for surgery, waiting for biopsy results, or even suffering from addiction or depression, you can receive the sacrament. Father Mellow says that Sunday that it's also given to people just because they're old, which is why he himself is receiving it today.

A few people get up from their pews, mostly old, some not, and the priests bless them with oil and lay their hands on their heads. A young priest whom I've never seen before lays his hands on Father Mellow's head, and sitting next to Sophia—who happens to be at the same Mass as me for once—I start snuffling. She silently passes me a Kleenex. Forgiveness and loving gestures in the church are sometimes a little hard for me to watch. I wonder if my grandfather, the practicing Catholic on my mom's side of the family, a gentle, incredibly sweet guy who nonetheless did thirty years in the FBI, chasing down bad guys with a gun in his hand, ever went through this before his health suddenly plummeted.

Waterworks week after week. Sometimes it's a hymn we sing; sometimes it's just reciting a prayer along with so many people; sometimes it's a homily; sometimes it's the sight of the sun arcing through the clerestory windows above the altar. But whatever is happening, I'm not used to it. Shaky and vulnerable, I go back to the Italian and tell him about the crying, and he nods, his cheeks pinking. "Maybe Jesus is telling you something," he says. "Maybe he wants you to know he is okay with you crying; maybe you're crying like Mary Magdalene. Because you're surprised by God."

Ignatian spirituality, he explains, is about "finding God in all things"; Jesuits and people who adhere to the Jesuit charism go through a series of meditations Saint Ignatius wrote in the sixteenth century, in which they meditate on the life of Christ in order to be able to bring Christ into their own lives and, by extension, into the lives of others. These meditations are called the "Spiritual Exercises," and the Italian tells me they're growing in popularity, even in our secular age. Many people do them on a month-long silent retreat along with a spiritual director; others do them in batches daily over the course of a year. They're not unlike basketball drills; ultimately all that sprinting and free throwing either makes you a better player, or you get sick of it and quit. In their sheer difficulty and rigor, the Exercises are befitting of the guy who invented them.

Ignatius is a very macho saint. Born in 1491 into a large family in the Basque town of Loyola, Spain, he grew into a small-time Lothario before joining the military. Fighting as a knight in battle, he was wounded when he took a cannonball to the leg (Damn, he was tough!), which required multiple surgeries without anesthesia and a long convalescence. While he was recuperating, he planned on reading more of the romantic novels he liked, which probably appealed to the ladies he was courting, but the place where he was staying only had copies of religious books.

Ignatius experienced his conversion while his bones slowly knit back together. He soon renounced all worldly goods and stopped cutting his fingernails and toenails for a time as a kind of penance. I gagged a little reading about that—I have a long-standing phobia of overly long toenails. Ignatius then took up a mendicant lifestyle, begging for change that he often gave away to even poorer beggars. He gathered a few companions, and they called themselves the Society of Jesus. Eventually he started cutting his toenails again, thanks be to God. The Society was quickly approved as a religious order by the pope at the time, who apparently found Ignatius's charism and personality appealing. The Jesuits grew into one of the world's largest religious orders and are today known especially for their roles as teachers, social justice activists, missionaries, and spiritual directors. They're all men; unlike other orders—Franciscans, Benedictines, Dominicans—they have no equivalent branch of nuns, though a few female congregations adhere to Ignatian spirituality. But, as a nun told me later, a lot of women don't like the Exercises; they're too regimented, and in some ways too militaristic, to appeal to the more emotional way of living with God that many women prefer.

Maybe I'm a dude at heart, because some part of Ignatius's oddball story appeals to me. Maybe it's the cannonball in the fucking leg—anybody who survived that and lived to march all the way from Spain to Jerusalem was one tough son of a bitch. But I'm not at that level of toughness in my spiritual life. I seem instead to be growing more gooey, more gelatinous, more sensitive. I try to explain this to the Italian during one of our sessions. The problem with the crying is that it's the antithesis of how I would like the world to perceive me. A lot of my writing is heavy on irony and sarcasm, laden with self-effacement, and frosted with a layer of bitterness. If I had a dollar for every time someone's told me I'm intimidating,

I wouldn't have to ever get up at 8 AM to explain semicolons again. So this wibbly-wobbly version of myself is one I'd rather leave behind. I'd rather be like Ignatius, I tell the Italian. "A badass." He laughs a little at that phrase and then rests his chin on his hands again. "If God is making you weak, you have to be okay with that," he says after a pause. "You know what Paul says, 'When I am weak, I am strong.'"

"Easy for Paul to say," I reply. "He had that thorn in the flesh as an excuse."

"Yes, but you have to remember: God doesn't want anybody to be angry all the time. It's okay to be vulnerable. This is all new to you. Why don't you write something about this?"

"Uh, no . . . I wouldn't want anyone to read that. I mean, my friends would probably think it was ridiculous."

"Why?"

"They think all Christians are fundamentalists, you know: we think everything in the Bible is literal; the world's only 6,000 years old; gay people are evil. The other day my husband asked if I thought he was going to Hell." This is true: Sage told me his biggest fear about my religious pursuits would be my turning into a raving evangelical who thinks all unbelievers are damned. I laughed and told him not to worry, but I didn't have any theological support for my claim that he was going to be fine in the afterlife.

"Jesus doesn't say unbelievers are going to Hell," the Italian says, shaking his head. "That's what fundamentalists think. He says it depends on how you treat poor people. Is your husband nice to poor people?"

"Well, he is a musician, so all his friends are poor . . . we're pretty broke . . . and he gives money to homeless people more often than I do . . ."

"So he's okay." He lifts his hands, palms up. "He's not going to Hell."

"I'll quote you on that." We smile at one another.

"But, Kaya. You should really write about this." He pauses for a moment, a flush creeping over his cheeks again. "Try to imagine yourself as Mary Magdalene. Write about why she cried."

"Yeah, okay, I'll try . . ."

"Just try. Writing is a gift, yes?" I resist the temptation to roll my eyes when I see how serious his expression is. "God wants you to use your gifts."

So over the next week I try to write something about faith. How it takes fucking forever. How disappointing it feels when a voice pipes up in my head during Mass, nagging me to just get up and go home. *It's 9 AM on a Sunday and everyone is in bed sleeping off their hangovers. What are you doing? You don't belong here. These people are much better Catholics than you'll ever be. They probably all think birth control was invented by Satan. Just get up. Walk out. Go home.* But I keep sitting there, listening.

Sometimes I am so self-conscious of my sinfulness, my unworthiness, that I feel like I must be leaving a slime trail behind me when I walk up for communion. I keep harping on the idea of sinfulness in my conversations with the Italian. This is clearly frustrating; he sends me home with gospel passage after gospel passage about Jesus forgiving sinners, but I keep coming back, saying that they weren't as sinful as me; after all, I have the modern world to assist me in my sins. Finally, in exasperation, he refers me to a movie.

"Do you know the movie *The Mission*?" he asks. I say no, I've never seen it; it looked goopy when I peered at a bit of it on TV.

"There's a scene in it, when De Niro, who's playing a slave-owner, kills his brother and goes to a priest—a Jesuit—to get forgiveness. The priest says, 'You killed someone. Take all your armor and swords, tie them to your back, and climb this waterfall. It's steep.' So De Niro does this. And he keeps doing it over and over again—he's really suffering—and one of the other priests cuts the cord to the bundle of armor. But De Niro, he picks up the cord, ties it around himself again. He keeps climbing and climbing until he meets the Indians he used to enslave. Then he knows whom to ask for forgiveness." I think about this story for a moment, but can't think of anything to say. "Kaya," the Italian says. "You keep tying your sins around yourself. You don't need to."

"I said something like that to myself on Easter," I reply.

"Well, you gave yourself good advice. You should listen to it."

We laugh about that. I realize that these conversations with the Italian are unlocking something else, something rougher and scarier than anything yet. They are unlocking my sense of belief.

However, there's a problem with seeing him and with talking about these matters in such depth. I realize what it is when I spend half an hour picking out which dress I'll wear, fidget with my hair in the car, reapply makeup and wonder if I'm showing too much cleavage, peer at the squint lines between my eyebrows. Halfway up the sloping block that leads to the Jesuit residence, I stop myself, look at the shoes I'm wearing, my painted toenails and freshly shaved calves. *Oh, God, it's finally happened*, I think. *You've got a crush on a priest.*

This is particularly embarrassing because in my thirty-eight years on earth, I have never had a crush on a teacher before, and now that I'm out of school for good, priests are the closest thing in my life to teachers. My favorite male professor in college was openly gay, a brave decision at a Catholic school. But I even used to do similarly girlie things before going to one of his classes. Not so that he'd be attracted to me, but to give myself some additional confidence. The sensations I'm feeling now—fluttering guts, my hand flying up to my mouth to cover my crooked teeth when I giggle inanely, thinking about things I want to tell him, raving about him to anyone who'll listen—all of it's not just mildly ridiculous; it makes me feel pathetic. Even my husband picks up on my mooning after the Italian pretty quickly and teases me about *The Thorn Birds* and presenting some sort of temptation to this guy. As if, I say. I look like a turnip on good days, I'm married, and besides, it's not like that.

And it isn't. It isn't *The Thorn Birds*, or any other stylized depiction of clerically directed lust. There's no sex in this equation: my crush on the Italian is not about his looks, because he is no big-nosed, skinny, tall guy of my typical type.

Nor is the crush about some sort of spiritual synthesis we've achieved through weeks of conversation. If anything, I think I leave him banging his head against the wall in frustration; my theological queries and stubborn insistence on evidence for everything are the opposite stuff to faith. I am not going to run off with this priest to Italy and start stomping grapes or something equally clichéd. Because my crush is really on God.

This sounds both tawdry and ridiculous, but think of it this way. You're a teenager, you're fumbly and greasy in your new body and face, and you have a creative temperament, so you might decide that you want nothing more than to be a painter. And then one day for the first time you meet somebody who is a serious painter, somebody who lives in a dingy studio and sleeps on a cot, eats nothing but Top Ramen and stays up all night, every night, painting and talking about painting with his painter-friends, and spends his days going to look at paintings. In retrospect, this guy sounds like bad news, but hear me out: He takes an interest in your painting, and he starts talking to you about it as if you have a legitimate chance of becoming a painter. So you spend some time learning from him, and then you start painting. And you fall in love with painting. It's something you feel like you were born to do. The painter was simply a conduit, a bridge that you needed to cross in order to get to what was on the other side, which was a way of expressing your oily and sweaty teenage self in a manner that just made a lot of fucking sense.

After talking with the Italian for a few weeks and cycling through most of my good outfits, it has become clear that re-entering Catholicism was not the biggest mistake of my life. The crying at Mass is beginning to make sense. My conversations with the Italian have revealed something I had not wanted to admit: in spite of my going through the motions with RCIA and weekly service, I have been holding faith at a comfortably intellectual distance. Or, as he put it, "You like to read about it, but you don't like to feel it."

Ignatius taught the Jesuits to end each day doing something called the Examination of Consciousness, or the examen. You start by acknowledging the fact that God is there with you; then you give thanks for the good parts of your day (mine usually include food); and finally, you spend ten minutes or so running through the events of the day from morning to the moment you sat down to pray, stopping to consider when you felt consolation, the closeness of God, or desolation, when you ignored God, or when you felt like God bailed on you. Then you ask forgiveness for anything shitty you did that day and for guidance tomorrow. If you do this every day, I guarantee you'll stop taking good stuff for granted. I spent most of my life saying thanks to people in a perfunctory, whatever kind of way. Now when I say it I really mean it, even if it's to the guy who makes those lattes I love getting in the morning, because I stopped and appreciated his latte skills the night before. If you are lucky and prone to belief, the examen will also help you start really feeling God in your life.

Part of this shift also comes about because I take the Italian's advice and start volunteering with the homeless. With its mild climate and relatively generous structure of food banks, shelters, and social services, Berkeley seems to have a particular profusion of homeless people. Over the years, I've developed a tactic of total avoidance. No eye contact. No acknowledgment. But it doesn't always work. The more I hear about caring for the poor during Mass, the worse I feel when I walk by a homeless person on the way to the car.

My church hosts a monthly dinner for the homeless, and it's a big production. Instead of a soup line, it's a sit-down meal for two hundred, with appetizers, salad, main course, cake, ice cream, entertainment, and a raffle. Serious work is involved; volunteers pull multiple shifts shopping, prepping, cooking, serving food, and cleaning. The first time I go, I'm shuttled into the kitchen by a harried young woman with a pen stuck into her ponytail, who asks me if I can lift heavy weights before putting me in front of two bins of potato salad and handing me an ice cream scoop. For three hours, I scoop potato salad onto plates, heft vats of potato salad, and scrape potato salad into the compost cans. I never want to eat potato salad again, but I also learn something about the homeless people I've been avoiding for years: some are mentally a mess, many—judging from the smell—are drunk off their asses, but on the whole, they are polite, intelligent, and more than anything else, grateful. As I walk back to my car, I'm stopped several times by many of them who want to thank me, saying how good the food was, how much they enjoyed it. "I didn't do anything," I say in return. "You were there," one of them replies.

The next time, I drag Sage along. He's asked to be a server, which means that between serving people he has to sit at the table with them and make conversation. "It's about *hospitality*," the Irish woman who's organizing people tells him. I get a glimpse of him now and then throughout the meal, and he seems to be enjoying himself; he's laughing with the guys at his table, sharing food, jumping up and heading to the kitchen for more water, clean forks, slices of cake. On the way home, I ask what he thought of it.

"It's funny," he says. "Two of the guys at my table were musicians. And they went to my high school."

"Did you know them back then?"

"No, they were a few years older. But still . . ."

And I think, there but for the grace of God we go. He's never had a problem with drugs or booze, but he watched his mother die from drinking, and meeting someone just a hair removed from his own circumstances who's wound up in a dire situation seems to have put him into a reflective frame of mind. He doesn't talk much for the rest of the day, but later he says, "I'd like to do that again."

An email soon comes from the women's shelter coordinator: if I can wake up at 5 AM, they need someone to cook. So I drag my half-awake ass up to Berkeley while it's still dark outside, buzz a hidden door that opens into a cramped room full of bunk beds and lockers, and crack and scramble seventy-two eggs (another food I never want to eat again) for the women in T-shirts and pajamas who shuffle up into a line to receive them. Many of them are recently homeless:

abuse, loss of a job, a million different stories. Some have kids who are navigating the impossibly complex shelter system along with them. On the first day, I meet a five-year-old in Elmo pajamas whose braids are coming undone. I'm there once a month and at the church meal once a month, and in between, when I see people I feed on the street, instead of focusing my eyes in the sidewalk and hoping they go away, we now have conversations.

My time with the Italian is running out. I knew from our first meeting that he would be leaving the United States, and perhaps that made me feel more comfortable asking him lots of ridiculous theological questions, weeping myself into a soggy mess, and dragging my burdens into the room. In a few days, he'll leave Berkeley and go back to Italy, stopping on the East Coast along the way to retrieve his stuff from the seminary where he'd been living before he came out here for the summer. "It's a lot of flying," he says. Jesuit formation is ridiculously long; they begin as novices for two years, and at the end of their novitiate, they're handed a minimal amount of cash (like $20) and told to make their way to their summer internships—usually in social justice ministries. Then they enter a long period where they're called Scholastics, and that's what they do: study, study, study. Many of them have multiple advanced degrees. Most are sent for additional time working in areas of extreme poverty and illness in Africa,

India, or Southeast Asia. By the time they're ordained, some of them have been in the order for fifteen years, which makes the English PhD candidates who linger in my building at Berkeley seem like total wimps in comparison.

The Jesuits then assign them a job, depending on their skills and interests. Lots of them teach; others go into ministry; some are writers, doctors, even scientists. The Italian was ordained at the Jesuit mother church in Rome last year and is now off to his first full-time assignment: teaching religious education to teenagers in Sicily. "High school students . . . I think they might kill me," he says with a smile. I tell him he'll be fine; I've taught teenagers for over a decade, and you simply have to clarify on the first day that cell phones are forbidden. That's more than half the work. We laugh about that and talk for a while about cell phones ringing at inappropriate moments during Mass. "Right when I raised the chalice!" he says with a laugh. "I had to roll my eyes to God."

The last time we meet, I ask him if it's okay to email him. "I'm interested in your life," I tell him, and it's true. I wonder what things will be like for him, if Sicily is as hot as they say, if he will like teaching. He says sure. "You know," he says in the final moments we spend together, "God is really working in your life." I laugh a little bit at that—sure, sure—and then I realize he's right. And I panic a little. What if God bails on me along with the Italian? Is the Italian going to keep a line to God open on my behalf? We only talked a little bit about all my issues with Church dogma—how am I going to handle that on my own? He walks me to the door, and we stand for a minute, the hot July wind blowing up from the Bay. "I hope you pray for me," he says. And I think, *Dude, of course I will.* "I'll pray for you," he adds. And I go to shake his hand, while he tries to give me a hug, and there's one of those awkward half-lunging bumbling moments, and I walk down the hill, toward home.

The crying in church tapers off as summer goes on. Every week, some ridiculous new edict erupts from the Vatican. Bishops are told not to report abuse cases to the police. Gay men are banned from entering the seminary. Vasectomies are declared "intrinsically evil." It starts to resemble white noise, all the backward gesturing, the fear of others. I stand in my pew during the consecration, praying for the Italian, praying for change in the Church he's a part of. *If there are others like him*, I think, *maybe it's not all so bad.*

I finally finish writing something about this whole messy faith journey, send off a query to a Catholic Web magazine that's not as egregiously pious as many of them, get a call from the editor, who says, "It's a fucking shitty thing that you felt so alienated, because it's about fucking belief" (told you Catholics swear). The essay gets published, and instead of a stream of comments calling me some sort of heretical loser, I hear from other alienated Catholics, wandering Catholics, Catholics whose faith was lost and found.

FIVE

For eight days, I've committed to going on an Ignatian retreat. Ever since the Italian and I did spiritual direction, I've been studying Ignatius's exercises and doing a daily examen, but nothing prepared me for what the retreat would turn out to be: my own personal desert experience. Part of my motivation to go was trying to puzzle out what kind of Catholic I would turn out to be. Historically, Catholics seem to fall into two categories. There are contemplatives like Thomas Merton, who meditate, keep silence, and tend to be more scholarly. Others, like Dorothy Day, are more active, diving into social justice, working with the poor, and trying to solve social problems at a grassroots level. I am neither and both, but the more I read about contemplation, the more it seemed like something that might do me some good. Although my anxiety has waned, holding a thought for more than two seconds, particularly a thought about God, is still beyond my capacity.

The retreat center itself is innocuous. Its buildings are the same sort of Spanish colonial style seen all over the West Coast, with sloping, red-tiled roofs and thick stucco walls. My room is located in a dormitory named after Saint Joseph, and a massive tile mural of him cradling a toddler Christ adorns one of its exterior walls. Joseph is usually depicted as middle-aged; the theory as to why he disappears from the gospel narratives is that he dies before Jesus begins his public ministry, but this Joseph is young and handsome, the baby Jesus cherubic and blond. When faced with cheesy religious art, one has to remember that the Holy Family were Palestinian Jews, because they are so often depicted looking like J. Crew catalog models.

The winding paths around the center lead to a series of brass plaques depicting the Stations of the Cross on one side, and a stone replica of Our Lady of Lourdes, standing before three stone children who look like cutesy Hummel figurines, on the other. Everything looks and feels as if it came out of the 1950s, and with many of the retreatants and resident priests sporting gray hair and walking canes, I imagine they've been coming here for that long or more. Even the food is straight out of *Leave It to Beaver*: meatloaf, Salisbury steak, bowls of tapioca pudding for dessert. Muggy air pollution hovers over the water below, and when I look out of the dining room windows, the entire place feels like it's encased in dusty amber.

Catholics have gone on retreats for a long time. Like everything else we do with any kind of ritualistic connotations, it's an exercise based on the gospels. I am frequently startled by the moments when Jesus suddenly bails on the disciples. "Jesus went away by himself to pray" is a refrain almost as commonly heard as the more enticing tales of miracles. Was the Son of Man kind of a jerk on occasion, or was he just burnt out? As with almost everything else in the Bible, "I don't know" is probably the best answer, but I've been cultivating a theory for a while.

According to the essay "Caring for Your Introvert" by Jonathan Rauch, introverts are solitary by nature but, frequently, also gifted performers. My secular saint heroes Bob Dylan and Leonard Cohen fit this bill. Introverts like small gatherings and conversation, but find parties exhausting, and often need time on our own to recover after attending one. "I think Jesus' bailing on the disciples means he might have been a classic introvert," I wrote to the friend who sent me Rauch's essay. Prayer and contemplation require long stretches of silence, and thus those who are drawn to these practices are oftentimes natural introverts. This is why quite a few orders of monks and nuns are cloistered: choosing a kind of permanent retreat, they abjure all contact with the outside world and head instead into what they see as the most direct line to God—a life that consists solely of prayer, spiritual reading, and physical labor.

But in the most sequestered orders, the attrition rates are staggeringly high. Confronted with nothing but God, many aspiring monks and nuns find themselves breaking down. There are no resident psychologists in monasteries, so people often vanish in the middle of the night, their memories just another ghostly presence in the hallways where God is murmuring. Some find long-term joy, but cloistered vocations are increasingly rare. In this age of information assault, very few people desire to completely withdraw from society, yet the occasional pull toward solitude, with its promises of being better able to hear God's voice, is irresistible.

Retreat centers give Catholics a chance to taste that kind of life on a short-term basis. Ignatius in particular designed the Spiritual Exercises to be done in a thirty-day stretch with three immersion days and three re-entry days on either end. Retreatants spend each day meditating on different episodes from the gospel and using their imaginations to place themselves in biblical scenes. They meet once a day with a spiritual director, but aside from that, they are not allowed to speak. It's a kind of spiritual marathon: grueling, isolating, often maddening, strangely addictive. Many people—religious and laypeople alike—return again and again for retreats. The retreat center I've come to offers both the thirty-day "long retreat," as they call it, and eight-day retreats for less durable spiritual athletes.

There are about fifty or so people making the long retreat congruously with my group, which arrives on a Sunday afternoon. When I get out of the car, I lean down to kiss my husband good-bye, and his worried expression reflects my own; both of us know how my solitary nature still requires bookstores, places to people-watch, and friends. "I'll call you if I go insane," I tell him. "Just don't become a nun," he replies, and I reassure him being married makes that impossible. Rolling my suitcase up to the registration center, I immediately notice how incredibly loud its wheels sound. There is no ambient noise: no car stereos pumping out heavy bass beats, no neighbors shouting in Spanish and Cantonese, no construction work. A man shuffles by, eyes to the ground, and I reflexively give him the pinch-lipped smile that makes me look constipated in photographs, but he doesn't look up. He just keeps shuffling. One of the priests checks me in and hands me a sheaf of paperwork: schedule of meals, Masses, map of the surprisingly large grounds, room information. And then I find a note that begins my journey down the spiritual rabbit hole. "The thirty-six-day retreatants and your fellow eight-day retreatants are not to be disturbed," it says. "Please respect their experience and refrain from greeting one another or making eye contact outside of Mass."

Eye contact is often difficult for me anyway, and friends and students have sometimes complained about this over the years, taking my wandering eyes as a symptom of disinterestedness, when in fact I'm usually looking away because I'm formulating a tricky thought. But the rule about not looking people in the eye at the retreat center is just weird. Even in Manhattan, where it feels like people are so stressed they'll punch you in the face if you say hello, I still look people in the eye on the street, across a café, in a museum. It's the most basic form of human contact. Walking past people looking down at the ground or gazing into some sort of awkward middle distance never ceases to be alienating to the extreme.

On the first evening we are allowed to talk for half an hour or so as part of our immersion, and I sit briefly with a handful of women, all elderly, who tell me they're regulars here, as we spear cheese cubes and sip ginger ale. These women have come back year after year for decades. One of them has even made the long retreat twice, which she swears is a life-changing experience. I nod and get up to grab some more cheese cubes, thinking thirty-six days would be insane; how could even the biggest loner survive that long without books, conversations, the consolations of friends?

Among the Carthusians, an order so austere that the monks are confined for the better part of each day to a small room with an attached walled garden known as a "cell," their days and nights are spent in absolute silence. But once a week they go out for a vigorous walk, during which they are not only encouraged but ordered to speak to one another, switching partners every half hour. Apparently this keeps them grounded in the knowledge that their brothers know who they are, which makes the long days in their cells more bearable. Before I came to the retreat house, I watched the documentary *Into Great Silence*, which chronicles the lives of Carthusians in their motherhouse, the Grande Chartreuse, located in the remote mountains of France. The movie is almost three hours long and true to its title, the only soundtrack is the ambient noise of the monastery—shuffling feet, frequently tuneless Gregorian chants (so much for the theory that all monks sing like angels—many of the Carthusians make Bob Dylan sound polished), the occasional bird call or rain shower. In one scene, the monks finally talk during their walk, and probably because they're cut off from all worldly news, they mostly make idle chitchat about life in the monastery. The biggest debate you overhear is whether or not they should use the Holy Water every time they enter the chapel—no doubt a hot-button issue in a religious order that likes to boast that it's "never deformed, never reformed." The monks have been living in exactly the same manner since their founding by Saint Bruno in the year 1084. The movie is beautiful, but so claustrophobia-inducing that I could only stand it in half-hour increments over a period of weeks, and every time a segment finished, I would burst out of my house and immediately drive to the neighborhood café so I could hear lots of loud music and inane urban hipster conversation.

As I'm putting more ice in my soda against the 90-degree-plus weather, a middle-aged guy with a swath of pure white hair starts chatting with me over the drinks table. As it turns out, he's here to discern whether or not he's going to become a deacon, a kind of demi-priesthood open to married men. Deacons assist at Mass and preach, and they can conduct funerals and marriages, but they can't consecrate the host and wine, baptize babies, or conduct the other sacraments. I know there were female deacons in the early Church who are even mentioned in Paul's letters, but they're not brought up often at Mass.

"I've never been away from my wife and kids for more than two days," the guy says, shifting his bottle of beer from one hand to the other so he can grab more chips. "It's going to be tough," he adds with a worried look.

"My husband's a musician," I respond. "He travels a lot. You get used to it." He nods.

"But my daughters are *teenagers*," he sighs, and I self-consciously glance down at a few of the tattoos that started appearing when I was still in high school, most likely on weekends when my own father was out of town.

At the end of this mixer we're sent off to dinner, where I talk with a white-habited nun from the Philippines who works as a schoolteacher, a Jesuit priest from Texas, an elderly nun who walks with a cane, and a nearly silent woman who, with some prodding, reveals that she's originally from Africa. It's an awkward dinner after an awkward mixer. Sure, it's nice getting to know these people, but after tonight's Mass we will not speak to one another again until the final morning of the retreat. And we're not even supposed to smile at one another again. One of the priests handed out a small card at orientation with everyone's names on it, "so you can pray for one another," but I can't match faces with names after one brief meeting, and these rather taciturn people I'm eating with have not revealed why they're here. The nuns and priest, I can guess: retreats are one of the few vacations they get to take, and as full-time spiritual seekers, they seem to be perfectly content with the idea of keeping silence. The African woman, I have no idea. She barely makes a sound, even when

I mention that one of my friends is from the same country as she is. She seems to already be winding down into the silence.

Mass follows dinner, and between the people making the long retreat, our group, and the large staff of priests and nuns, there isn't much elbow room in the small chapel. There is, however, air conditioning, which I take note of because the forecast is predicting a lot of very warm days and my room has only a torpid ceiling fan. As it turns out, one of the priests who runs the center composes church music and makes frequent appearances at the Mass, strumming a guitar and leading us all through the kind of folk-rock church anthems I grew up singing.

On the first night, we do an upbeat rendition of a number by the St. Louis Jesuits, kind of a holy-geek version of Peter, Paul, and Mary. The service is short, with the priest plowing through the gospel reading at high speed, delivering a truncated homily, and leading a rapid-fire line at communion. This is the first time I've glanced at the people making the long retreat, who were separated from us at the first dinner but with whom we'll take meals for the rest of the week. A poster board with their photos and names in the lobby reveals they're mostly from religious orders: lots of young nuns, all of them in long flowing habits; a couple of young guys in brown robes and sandals who turn out to be Carmelite monks, which is the first time I've ever seen anyone from that order, since it's primarily cloistered. Another guy in a brown robe is not a Carmelite but a Franciscan. There are a few priests in street clothing, and a dozen or so laypeople, mostly middle-aged or older, one of whom has skinny braids in her hair that hang over her eyes and is wearing the kind of baggy purple cottony dress and Birkenstocks that make me ninety-nine percent sure she's from Berkeley or some place very much like it.

After Mass I go back to my airless room, crank the ceiling fan up to its rather pathetic high speed, open the small window, sit on the bed, and think . . . shit. My phone is at home, but I've brought my laptop in order to do some writing, and yes, there is wireless. But I force myself not to check email or the news, even though the high-profile trial of the transit cop who shot an Oakland kid in the back is scheduled to wrap up while I'm here, and everyone back home is freaking out about possible looting and rioting. The only thing to do about that, I guess, is to pray. Saint Romuald, who founded the Camaldolese order, told the monks to "sit in your cell as if in paradise." Repeating this phrase a few times, my knees digging into the warm, abrasive carpet where I'm sitting, I wait for God to start talking. After a long two minutes, nothing happens. Mental chatter begins as abruptly as my butt hits my heels. "Lame," I say to myself, and get up and walk around the grounds, remembering to jerk my eyes down to my feet whenever someone walks by.

It's the Fourth of July, and some of the nuns and the two Carmelite monks are sitting on the benches near the entrance, waiting for the sun to descend so they can get a glance at the fireworks. I note that one of the monks seems to actually be embroidering, holding one of those round embroidery wheels that my grandmother used to spend hours and hours poking a needle into. He is actually a pretty cute young guy, probably still in his twenties, with dark eyebrows and close-cropped hair. Against all rules of the retreat center, he looks up and into my eyes for minute as I'm passing by, and his expression is so serious, so lacking in any opening for communication, that I almost jerk backward. Someone is actually hearing God, I think as I skid back toward my room. Lucky fucker.

The terrible night's sleep that always occurs in an unfamiliar, too small bed takes me into the next day until the predawn light seeps through the window and I stumble to the dining room to fill my coffee cup, and then stumble back to the room. After repeating this ritual several times and taking a shower, it's time to meet my spiritual director. Father Godot and I met briefly last night at the mixer, and part of the reason I wanted to work with him was because his long, thin face, beaklike nose, and spiky white hair make him look startlingly like Samuel Beckett. But unlike the famously bleak and cranky writer, Father Godot is chill. He dresses casually, in a hoodie on cold mornings or a guayabera on warm ones. Like Father Mellow, he exudes calm and patience, and he has long, slender hands that he frequently employs in exuberant gestures, which is a nice distraction when you're sitting for an hour getting heavy into theology and spiritual matters. After just one evening of silence, I am ready to talk with just about anyone about anything.

Father Godot's office, which is dim from the shutters being pulled against the morning sun, is full of pigs. The shelves are lined with stuffed animals, pig statuettes, pig greeting cards, and pig souvenirs. An entire corner of the room is piled with pigs. Just as I'm sitting down, one of them starts squealing. "Battery's running low," he explains. "Okay, I have to ask . . . about the pigs," I reply with a bit of hesitation. Lots of priests are eccentric, but this is pretty damn odd. "I had a heart valve replacement years ago," he says, patting his slender chest. "They put a pig valve in my heart and people latched onto that."

Like a lot of priests, Father Godot worked for years as a high school teacher before coming here to help run the retreats. I tell him about the years I spent teaching at a Catholic college before landing my job at Berkeley, and we make small talk for a while about Catholic schools and the kinds of kids who end up at them. But eventually he asks why I'm here. "Most people come for these longer retreats because they're working on something particular," he says. "The guy coming in after you, he just retired and he's trying to figure out what to do with his life. Or maybe they're figuring out a vocation." "Um, no, neither of those," I admit. And out tumbles the story again: Kaya Oakes, radical returning Catholic and full-time skeptic. Ask me about birth control, women's ordination, and other heretical topics of your choice. "Okay," he says cheerfully. "Nothing specific." Then he pauses for a minute and looks me in the eye. "But you know," he says in a lower voice, "I'm a Vatican II guy." And I smile. Another priest used this phrase with me once before. It often appears in articles and books by priests. If you're a priest and a Vatican

II guy, it means you are definitely not a Benedict guy, and probably not a John Paul II guy either. You're a John XXIII guy, and that means your Catholicism is about a Church that needs to keep moving forward instead of jerking backward by increments. And that's enough to make me trust Father Godot.

He gives me some Bible passages to read, bits from the Book of Hosea, a few pages from Luke, "good stuff for beginning a retreat," and like every other legendarily longwinded priest in his order, goes over the time limit for our session. When I open the door, the next retreatant is anxiously pacing the hallway outside, probably worried that he's lost his turn.

The first few days of the retreat proceed in much the same fashion. Wake at dawn, stumble to get coffee, stumble back to room, attempt to meditate, give up after two minutes, walk the grounds, shower, walk some more, eat some sort of carb-heavy, meaty lunch, read, nap, walk some more, attend Mass, eat dinner, walk some more. Other people seem to be staying in their rooms all day, because many of my walks are deserted. The woman in the room next to me arrived with boxes of books and art supplies, and I only glance her in the morning when I'm on coffee runs. Some people get into their cars each morning and drive off in a cloud of dust, only to suspiciously return around dinnertime. I pass the deacon guy now and then, and his expression is inevitably one of downcast worry; the Bible he's always holding flutters with ribboned bookmarks. The nuns are always in the chapel, taking turns in front of the tabernacle. This is called Eucharistic Adoration, and it's an old tradition; cloistered nuns and monks spend hours kneeling and praying in front of the pile of consecrated hosts. It's as if they are so focused on being near the body of Christ that they can't get up and go look for him in other people. The practice has never appealed to me, so every time I go to the chapel and see the nuns kneeling there in flawless white habits with long black veils and long black rosaries, I turn around and walk out again. God hasn't said a damn thing to me yet.

The nuns are everywhere. In the chapel at all hours of the day and night, taking turns kneeling in front of the circular brass tabernacle that glows like a dingy spaceship. On the paths with epically long rosaries swinging from their belts down to their knees, weaving flower garlands as they walk, and placing them on the head of the stone Virgin. Sitting on the courtyard benches, their stilled hands grasping Bibles. Eating in the dining room, eyes locked on their plates.

On the third morning Father Godot and I sit across from one another, and I tell him the nuns are freaking me out. It's not that I've never been around a nun; it's just that these particular nuns are all young, wearing habits, with the kind of pious facial expressions you normally see only on a holy card. "Well, don't be afraid of them!" Father Godot says, laughing a little. "They won't hurt you." He leans back and knits his spindly fingers together. "But it's so hot," he sighs. "I just wish they'd take off their veils now and then, they look so miserable. I just look at them and think, you could just slide it back . . ."

And it is hot. Hot like the dust lingers in the air as I pound my way around the retreat center's property, my steps banging out arcs in the dirt to recompense for the fact that I've voluntarily surrendered my right to speak other than the hour a day I spend with Father Godot. Hot like tank tops at dinner time, the chapel the only air-conditioned room, the paper-thin walls of my tiny room absorbing heat all day and returning it throughout the night as the nun in the room next door and the friar in the room underneath snore so loudly the water glass on the bedside table quivers and I roll over and over and over in the miniature bed with its abrasive sheets. It's hot, no one is allowed to speak, the nuns are everywhere, and it's only been three days so there's no way I can give up and go home.

Father Godot asks me what bothers me about the nuns, and it's easy to pinpoint: "They make it look so . . . easy!" I say, biting back the "fucking" that I'd normally interject. "God is *always* talking to them, isn't he? It's like, God's on the line 24/7 and they're just so . . . *holy!*" To Father Godot's credit, he doesn't remind me that being holy's their job, he just sits back and looks a little bit sad. "I'm going crazy here," I continue, finally admitting it. "God isn't talking; Jesus isn't talking; nobody's talking to me. There are no *signs*. Everybody here looks like they're in tune with God all the time and I can't stand it. He's just . . . ignoring me. What did I do?"

Father Godot keeps looking sad for a minute, and I think, *Shit, maybe I overdid it.* It's his job to be holy all the time too. But his Beckettian face is not judgmental or pitying; he's looking at me with compassion.

"It's not easy coming here," he says, and then reminds me that without a specific intention, I have to work harder to figure out what it is that I'm after or else the Exercises and all the prayers and readings won't work. For the rest of the hour, we try to figure out what I'm after. Silence, I tell him. "Supposedly it makes it easier to hear God." Not always, he says. It makes it harder for some people, "especially with the lack of eye contact. Personally, I don't like that practice, but the guy in charge does." He mentions Dorothy Day as the opposite of a contemplative and I perk up a little bit, because Dorothy is one of my heroes; she was an anarchist, and a writer, and she spent much of her time talking and listening to people. Even Teresa of Avila, the Spanish mystic saint, left her cloister and spoke up, he mentions, and now she's a Doctor of the Church. "Everybody needs a balance," he says. "Not gonna happen here," I mutter. "You know, it's not a prison," he says, folding his hands and leaning back. "If you need to go into town, go into town. It's fine."

I'm beyond frustrated by this point, my inner monologue raging on and on. Last night at dinner, I left my sweater on a chair while I went to get food, and returned to find an elderly lady yanking the chair out of my hand. Unable to make eye contact or speak, we launched into a brief tugging match before I let go, mentally unleashing an Oakland-style tirade about crabby old bitches as I wandered off to find a different seat. "Probably she's been in that seat for a million years and now she hates me," I tell Father Godot. "I'm such a mess." "Go into town," he says. "Take a break." As I'm heading toward the door, he stops me. "Maybe you're not as much of a mess as you think."

Town is a posh, quaint suburb, about a half-hour walk downhill though a subdivision until the hill flattens out into a lush green landscape, populated by tech millionaires and their blonde and buffed wives in yoga gear, the yards carefully tended by Mexican gardeners. From sprinklers running all day, priceless water hisses away to nothing on concrete curbs. Priuses silently sweep by, SUVs that could house an entire family and their nannies barrel by, guys wearing ridiculous spandex outfits on bicycles that cost more than my monthly paycheck whiz by, but I'm the sole pedestrian. Rage is seething through me until I can feel my blood pressure mounting. Blood throbs through my temples and I clench and unclench sweaty fists. What was the point of this expensive retreat that cost me nearly $1,000 I can ill afford? What made this seem like a good idea? *Fail, fail, fail, fail, fail* go my footsteps in this bucolic, fake landscape.

Sage picks up the phone back home. "It's not working," I bleat, standing outside of the local drugstore, where I've just overheard the cashier berating a mailman, a jarringly loud argument after days of silence. I just stood numbly by with my handful of purchases until it ended. I keep whining into my cell phone. "It's full of nuns and they keep serving meatloaf and everybody's looking at their feet and they're all holy. I miss Oakland. I even miss gangster rap." He listens to my disjointed ranting for a while, and asks if I want to come home. "I paid for this shit!" I reply. "Everybody's hearing God all the time and I can't hear a fucking thing!" "Give it time. Call me if you need anything," he says. He's been through this before, the rants I go on and their lack of logic. We move on to other topics—music he's working on, the possible riots that are about to break out in Oakland because of the high-profile trial, weird stuff our cats are doing. The iron bands around my skull start to loosen a little. "I have this weird urge to go shopping," I admit. There's a shoe store across the street, which is my favorite thing next to a bookstore, and he laughs. "You're not a nun," he says, and he's right. After we hang up, I try on some shoes, prying my swollen feet into vertiginous heels, impractical sandals, things that make my feet look like pudgy hookers. It's a beautiful thing to see.

Back at Mass that evening, the reflection is delivered by one of the nuns who's directing the long retreat, a Sister of Mercy in a polo shirt and khakis. It is not typical for a woman to preach in the Catholic Church. Women are restricted not only from ordination but also from delivering the gospel. A few bishops and priests look the other way, but it's not permitted to call what a woman delivers a homily, even if she's in holy orders like this Sister of Mercy; her talk must be referred to as a "reflection."

As usual when there's a female speaker, I sit upright. Like many Mercy Sisters, she works as a nurse, and she relates the story of a young man, dying of cancer, and his mother, who'd come to read to him from Mark's gospel. Even though he was past the point of comprehension, she read it to him because that's what he asked her to do when he was diagnosed. Relating this back to the gospel reading, when Jesus is curing yet another afflicted person, she talks about the nature of faith, how often Jesus tells the person he's cured not to run and spread the word. That's because Jesus only wants to cure people who really trust him, she says. But as a nurse, she knows that not every believer gets cured like the blind man or the woman with the hemorrhages. Some sick people just get sicker and eventually die. And almost nobody rises up out of his or her grave like Lazarus. Maybe the cure is really a lesson in trust. Heaven doesn't have to be angels tooting around on clouds. Christ is teaching us that faith is more about trusting that God will be with you at your very worst, and that when you die you'll feel a sense of great love.

Father Godot is in clericals the next morning, his black suit and Roman collar enhancing the thinness of his frame. Twice a week, he drives into town and says Mass for a monastery of cloistered Poor Clare nuns. "Their whole life is penitence,"

he says, looking a little worn around the eyes. "Not all the Poor Clares are like that, but . . . you know, I'm not a Passionist," he tells me. I must look confused, because he explains that some Catholics so identify with the suffering, dying Christ that their entire way of life becomes wrapped up in that. *Mel Gibson*, I think, but keep my mouth shut. Father Godot explains that there are many other ways of relating to Christ: the redemptionist view, in which you focus your faith on salvation; the focus on healing lived out by so many vowed religious who minister to the sick; missionaries, who do social justice work in impoverished places; and what he calls "the people who have the gift of tongues." "Writers?" I say. "But we're such skeptics." "Sometimes that's a good thing," he replies.

Skepticism is so much the opposite of how everyone around me seems to believe. Lifelong Catholics take a lot for granted. When they say the Creed, they either mean every word of it—*We believe in one God, the Father Almighty*—or they're mumbling through it just to get to the end—*We look for the resurrection of the dead and the life of the world to come, Amen*—but either way it's an intrinsic part of who they are. Given the content of the reading at Mass last night, I am still having trouble wrestling with the concept that Jesus wasn't just the Son of God but was also a man: one who walked around, went to the bathroom, ate dinner, had crushes and arguments. Father Godot finds this unusual. "Most people have an easy time relating to Jesus as human. Think about the storm on the sea, when all the apostles are asleep on the boat. What's Jesus doing?" I try to remember this one. "He's sleeping too." "Exactly. And they wake him up"—Father Godot jerks his head around like somebody pulled out of sleep—"and what happens after that? He waves his hand, calms the storm, and probably goes back to sleep." I laugh a little. Jesus takes naps.

Although my rage is beginning to ease, a state of near-constant discomfort still trails me around. The bed sucks, and I sleep badly. The nun next door and the friar below continue to snore like dragons. The buffet line leads me to overeat, which makes me feel dully bloated. Everyone still looks so damned holy, as if they should be floating half a foot off the ground, and the heat makes me puffy, oily, and grouchy. In this state of agitation, the last thing I'm capable of is relating to Christ.

On the fifth day, we're invited to a healing service, which is a chance for people to go say confession if they want, with a Mass beforehand. While I'm sitting there debating about making confession, someone taps me on the shoulder. I turn halfway and look into the eyes of one of the priests. He has a sweet, round face with a beard, and asks, "Do you ever distribute Eucharist?"

"Um, no," I reply. Father Mellow suggested I try it, but I'm such a germaphobe that it grosses me out.

"Well, would you mind doing it tomorrow night at Mass? You just give people the cup and say, 'Blood of Christ.' Just watch what other people are doing."

"Um, yeah, okay." He pats my shoulder and vanishes.

"I got a tap on the shoulder," I tell Father Godot the next morning, and explain what happened. He says the priests take it for granted that most of the people who come here participate a lot in their churches and have experience with things like that. He also reminds me to wipe the rim and then rotate the cup each time. "What about if there's stuff left in the bottom?" I ask. "Oh, just leave it on the side, the priest will take care of it," he replies. Because it's the blood of Christ, you're not supposed to throw it away; someone has to drink it, usually the priest. However, since I'm the kind of person who can barely deal with shaking hands at Mass, the first time I watched a priest swigging the backwash of hundreds of communicants, I nearly vomited in my pew. Now, it's just routine, but I still shudder and hug myself when I see it happening.

Don't drop it, don't drop it, don't drop it is my marching refrain that evening, as I drag my feet toward the altar and shakily take a glass of consecrated wine. Along with two of the habited nuns and a middle-aged woman from my retreat group, I stand up front, can't remember if you can look people in the eye for this part or not, hold it out, mumble, "Blood of Christ," wipe, rotate. I look up to see the snoring friar who's been keeping me up at night standing in front of me. He walks around most days in shorts and a T-shirt, but changes into his rough-spun, rope-belted Franciscan robe at Mass. When our eyes meet, I probably grimace from nerves, but he smiles, and his face, weathered and bearded, with protruding teeth and beetling eyebrows, is transformed into the most beautiful thing I've seen all week. *God, forgive me*, I think as the friar hands the cup back to me. Comparing myself to all these devout Catholics has made me into a rotten-tempered bitch.

The nuns, the other laywoman, and I all shuffle over to the side table to put down our glasses, but the nuns stop and drink the remaining wine out of theirs. The laywoman follows suit. Then, to my horror, they go even further. They take a little carafe of water, pour it in, swish it around and drink that too. Oh my God, I am going to vomit in front of everyone, I think, but I lean my head back and pound the wine down. I really don't want these nuns to think I'm some sort of apostate. Then I put the water in and drink that too. On the way back to my pew a list of orally transmitted diseases skirls through my mind: flu, colds, mono, Hantavirus, Norwalk virus, the plague.

Dinner goes down like a pebble falling into a roaring ocean, because my stomach is apparently attempting to vacate my body via my nose. But the vomit never comes up, and I never get sick. It is a sacrament, after all. Then I recall something Rachel said back in RCIA when I mentioned that I dislike drinking wine at communion because of the backwash thing. "That doesn't worry me," she said. "I just figure, it's church."

Two days before the end of the retreat, I'm sitting on a bench in the courtyard before Mass, paging through the Book of

Hosea, the story of a man whose wife becomes a prostitute. The Old Testament is dirty, I think, and pick up my pen to scrawl a few notes. A shadow passes over me, and I look up to see the African woman whom I sat with at dinner on the first night, standing only a few inches away. She's wearing the same white shirt and black pants she seems to have had on for the entire retreat, and she's looking right into my face. Her expression is hard to describe: she looks terrified, but also like she's pleading for something. Against the rules, I mouth, "Are you okay?" and smile, but she just keeps standing there, staring at me. I've certainly seen enough homeless women snap at the shelter, but paralysis sets in. What can I do? I can't talk to anyone and when I say, "Are you okay" out loud in a whisper, she doesn't reply. I smile again, get up, and go try to find Father Godot, who's not in his office. When I return to the courtyard, she is now standing and staring at someone else, shaking slightly now. Mass is about to begin, and people are filing by, not looking at her, because that's against the rules. I have no idea what to do for her.

She's the last in line for communion, and when she's offered the host, she just stands there. "Body of Christ? Body of Christ?" says the Eucharistic minister, holding it out to her, but she won't take the host, and she eventually goes back to her pew empty-handed. A few minutes later at dinner, she wanders into the dining room after people have begun eating, and walks up to one of the Carmelite monks. After she's stood there staring at him for a few minutes, he asks out loud, "Do you want some food?" but she doesn't reply, doesn't even shake her head. She just stands there. And while a few people have finally begun to look up from their food, the vast majority of them ignore her. That's it, I think, I have to go get somebody, but as soon as I stand another woman comes, puts her arm around the now-catatonic woman, leads her outside, and sits holding her hand and talking to her softly. Another guy in my retreat group and I stand outside, and I ask if somebody went to get help. "She needs a priest . . . she needs help," he replies, and sure enough, Father Godot and one of the other priests arrive, ushering her into an office. She vanishes for the rest of the night, but I'm shaken like I've witnessed a particularly violent traffic accident. No matter how many times I've fist-fought the Noonday Demon, no matter how many times I've choked on a panic attack, I have never snapped like this woman just snapped, completely severing herself from the reality of these strange and silent surroundings.

The next morning, I ask Father Godot what happened, and he sighs unhappily. He looks like he hasn't slept. They took her to the emergency room, but she refused to be admitted. The doctors gave her some kind of sedative, but nobody is answering at the emergency contact numbers listed on her application form. There's nothing they can do. "We just have to pray for our sister," he says, and the sadness and frustration are clear in his voice. It must be hard when a priest realizes that he can't save somebody. And right then, looking at Father Godot and realizing that my time here is almost over and that this poor woman isn't going to get better and there's nothing I can do, I know it is time to go home. I tell him that, and we spend the rest of the hour on small talk. Chitchat fills the spiritual void that has been underneath me this entire week, which has suddenly grown so wide that I know staying here would lead me to tumble straight into it. I promise to send him some articles I've written, but my writing has never felt more phony. Here I am trying to write about spirituality, and in an entire week of restless meditation and fruitless prayer, God never revealed himself to me, not even once, not even for a second. Ignatius says we either spend our days in consolation, feeling and knowing the presence of God, or in desolation, when we feel the absence of God, most likely by turning away from God. What that woman displayed in her delirium was desolation to the extreme. In this place where the silence purportedly helps us to hear God even more loudly, perhaps she too tried and failed to discern what he wanted for her. Or maybe she was simply ill and unmedicated. Either way, it is time to go home.

I take the train to pick up my car from the parking lot where Sage has left it, and driving through downtown Oakland, I see windows boarded up against the riot everyone worried would happen. The transit cop was convicted only of involuntary manslaughter and will barely see a year behind bars even after shooting an unarmed man in the back, but when the verdict came down, the city did not burn. It only smoldered, the sense of injustice causing a few downtown windows to crack with the force of the people who knew that the system had failed them and would fail them again and again and again.

I wonder if the nuns know about Oscar Grant, the dead kid, or about Johannes Mehserle, the transit cop, just under thirty years old. I wonder if either of their families, holed up in their homes, feel any sense of consolation. I wonder if Christ walked with them at the funeral.

SIX

Elizabeth's buzzer is confusing and involves punching in codes and pound signs and a deafening *blaaaat*, and since we've never met before, things are complicated by the fact that three other women push their way through the door behind me so that Elizabeth, standing at the top of the stairs, has to pick me out among them. But I recognize her because I've worked for her. She coordinates the volunteers at the church homeless meals, is a lector and Eucharistic minister, and makes announcements about the parish council at Mass, and thus is the sort of Catholic that makes other Catholics feel . . . *bad.* Guilty for not doing more.

I take a seat next to Sophia, who's got a sprained ankle propped up on the table. Across the room is Margaret, with long legs and a flawless manicure, wearing a leather jacket and jeans. I recognize her from Mass, and soon learn that in contrast to her outspoken personality, she's a former contemplative nun. On my other side is Agnes, with a broad smile and a glittering scarf around her neck, also a former nun, from an order that works among the poorest of the poor. Elizabeth, with curly dark hair and leaping hand gestures, is wearing red and getting everyone water, and it turns out that she too briefly lived in a convent after she finished high school. As they introduce themselves, more details are forthcoming: Margaret is retired and has been with her female partner for twenty-five years; Agnes is a theology professor and writer, with two kids in college; Elizabeth works for an educational program and volunteers everywhere. I am, by decades, the youngest woman there.

Ten years ago, it began at Masses, they tell me. These women, who knew one another via various ministries, kept saying to one another after the Mass that it "wasn't enough." Sure, women got up and read from the Bible, but otherwise, they weren't visible on the altar. "So I went to the pastor at the time," Agnes says, "and said, women make up the majority of this congregation. You ought to think about letting us speak now and then." Surprisingly, he went for it, and ever since then, women have delivered reflections at our church.

Some of those women decided that it still wasn't enough, so one of them, who was teaching at theological school and studying female mystics and contemplative prayer communities, suggested a monthly gathering: a time to share experiences—good and bad—as Catholic women, and a time to reflect. This is what Sophia referred to as "pray and bitch." Also, they decided there should always be dessert.

There is an established intimacy among these women that is, at first, a little daunting. Any time you enter a room full of people who've been talking to one another for a decade, there is going to be a period when you spend most of your time simply listening. So that's what I do. I hear what they're saying about faith, about the priests at our church and how they relate to women, about the bishops and cardinals above the priests and how they ignore women, about the things they are reading and thinking about. And I realize several things in rapid succession: you can be Catholic and feminist. You can be Catholic and lesbian. You can be Catholic and a straight female and not have kids. You can be Catholic and have children but wonder if they should be Catholic. You can be Catholic and believe in better access to birth control, especially in impoverished and AIDS-ravaged communities. You can be Catholic and female and not be a nun and still be a leader in the church. Women, as it turns out, are part of the priestly class. It's just that they aren't allowed to minister publicly. They do it in places like here, and in hospitals, classrooms, homeless shelters, and in any room, really, where there is someone who needs healing.

The pray-and-bitch routine: First, somebody (this night it's Margaret's turn) produces some sort of food for thought, usually a reading, and then everyone meditates silently for a while. Squirmy and terrible at meditating, I feel like this goes on forever, when in reality, it's probably twenty minutes.

After that, everyone talks about what came up while they were meditating, we read a Psalm together, and then we eat dessert: tonight, some sort of poppyseed cake.

And then we bitch. Sophia had told me before that these women were deeply faithful but their faith butted up against the same things mine did: the Church stances on issues related to women, whether that meant our lack of leadership roles or the idea that birth control was always wrong. Earlier that week, I'd gone to daily Mass, something usually impossible given my teaching schedule, but it was the feast of Mary Magdalene so I'd made the extra effort. I tell these women that while Father Mellow did a nice little homily about her, it bothered me that it wasn't delivered by a woman; after all, wasn't Mary Magdalene a leader in the early church? "Of course she was," Agnes replies. And that leads to another conversation about why women aren't seen as leaders, even in a modern church where women in the surrounding secular world can run corporations, families, and countries just fine. And I think, yes. There has been something missing from this experience of Catholicism that I've plunged into to such a surprising depth. It's the women.

I have three sisters, all of whom possess what their husbands politely refer to as "big" personalities. Family gatherings usually consist of a lot of women talking over one another, often at near-deafening volume. Oakes women are not exactly the type to sit around waiting for some man to tell them what to do, perhaps because our father was cowed by having so many daughters and spent many nights attempting, and failing, to get us to follow orders. We all work, and we all work our asses off. We all married guys who have to put up with us, and we don't exactly follow orders: we give them. The men in our lives are pretty good about meeting us halfway, but sometimes I feel bad for them, including my brother and father. It's like a tidal wave of estrogen and cursing hit them and they just have to keep paddling to stay afloat.

So the masculine hierarchy of the Church, and its repeated failure to open its doors to the voices of some very powerful theological thinkers who happen to be female, has always felt like a foreign environment. However, I like a challenge, and while one is not exactly encouraged to shout back protests during the Mass when the priest slips up and says, "Blessed is he who comes in the name of the Lord" (that *should* be "blessed is the ONE who comes, not HE"—Hello, do you SEE all these women in the pews, dude?), the occasionally bossy and frequently ignorant things the big *C* Church says about women give me something to struggle against and educate myself about. It's like politics for liberals. Republicans and Tea Partiers may repulse us, but oppositional sides have their purpose. They give us something to struggle against.

I regularly direct prayers at Mary Magdalene, Teresa of Avila, Dorothy Day, and other kick-ass intercessors, so women have been in my faith life, but this is the first time I've ever sat on a hard couch in a dim apartment with them talking about what the Church should look like and what it could be. There's a reason that female Christian mystics specialized in visions. Women are good at constructing idealized scenarios, whether in the books we write or the dream lives we drift into while conscious or unconscious. These women in the room are talking about everything: people in their own lives who are suffering, global poverty, local politics, the homily delivered at Mass. But they are doing it all through a lens focused not on how everything is broken, but on ways to repair it all.

After Christ died, we know that the Church, such as it was, was small. People knew one another intimately and held Masses in one another's homes, or in caves, or any place where they could worship away from the prying eyes of Roman authority. And from the Acts of the Apostles we also know that many of the leaders and participants in these small communities were women. Thus the pray-and-bitch group hearkens back to the earliest days of the Church. Today in many large parishes, like ours, there is little to no connection happening between the people in the pews. Sure, you may see the same people every week, but no conversation occurs beyond "Peace be with you." The idea of community is highly elusive, and before I sat with these women, the idea of finding a feminist Catholic community seemed like a joke.

In a Catholic Mass, there's a part called "Prayers of the Faithful." The lector gets up and asks people what they want to pray for. Usually, this ends up being some mishmash of social justice issues: poverty, the recession, war, famine, and so on. And sometimes people get personal, asking the church to pray for a dying parent or a sick child. In the years I've attended Mass, I've only heard someone pray "for the culture of life" once, and it took me a minute to understand what they were talking about: abortion and euthanasia. As we all know, the Vatican takes a pretty hard line on both of those issues, and it's one of the chief reasons for the attrition of many liberal Catholics. But one of the rather open secrets about Catholicism is that plenty of Catholics don't toe the line as hard as the Vatican does. Each Catholic examines her conscience, and if her conscience says that an abortion done to save the life of the mother keeps at least one person alive, or if a condom worn by a guy with AIDS keeps AIDS from spreading, or if a cancer-racked body needs to depart the world painlessly, then so be it. The God we believe in, after all, is a God of mercy and compassion.

This was reinforced at a daylong retreat in the Northern California mountains I went to just before meeting the pray-and-bitch ladies. At dinnertime, I was sitting next to a woman in her sixties. She was a psychiatric intake nurse in a large public hospital in San Francisco, an unbelievably tough job in a city with a large population of homeless people, many of whom struggle with untreated mental illness and drug addiction. We got to talking about the difficulties of being married while working high-stress jobs, and when she asked me if I had kids, I braced myself for the textbook Catholic reaction: You're supposed to have kids! God gave you a uterus! But when I said, "No, I've never felt a calling to motherhood," she nodded and said, "Me neither. And aren't we blessed to live in a time when we have that choice?" Momentarily, I glanced around to make sure we were still on a Catholic retreat, and then gave her a grateful smile.

But not every Catholic woman is that compassionate and open-minded. There is an elderly woman who shows up now and then at daily Masses at my parish, who was there on the feast day of Mary Magdalene. During the prayers of the faithful, she tends to shout, not speak. And she always shouts the same thing: "Let us pray for an END to abortion." And I always cough. The problem is not that she believes what she believes—whether I agree or not, she is entitled to her opinion—the problem is that she yells it in a quiet church when people are trying to hear God, not a cranky person with a vendetta.

That's the primary problem with the more vocal and occasionally violent wing of the pro-life movement. Rather than approaching the issue with any modicum of compassion or understanding for the women who find themselves facing an unwanted pregnancy, rather than listening to what reasonable, well-educated people have to say on the topic, they scream and damn them to Hell. I don't believe that most women look forward to having abortions or treat them in any sort of cavalier manner; there should probably be fewer of them, because there should also be greater access to birth control and sex education, especially for women who live in poverty. Yet some right-wing Catholics will say things like the earthquake and tsunami in Japan that killed thousands was punishment from God for the Japanese approving the morning-after pill. Or they'll take to the Internet and write swaths of vitriol that are so damning that reading them makes me break out in rage sweat. The yelling abortion lady at Mass makes me wish I'd stayed home.

Yanking her foot off of the coffee table and leaning forward, Sophia says that instead of yelling about abortion, perhaps we should be yelling that women deserve compassion. And we all agree that the Church is not very good at that. Yet it is good at many other things, and that's the dilemma: these women are all cradle Catholics; three are former nuns; and all of them love the Mass, the sacraments, social justice, and Christ. Yet, as we talk, their stories often make it feel like the Church does not love women back unless they are nuns (and as I later learn from a few nuns, not so much then either) or the Virgin Mary, and some priests go into the seminary too young; they never establish deep friendships with women, and thus fail at understanding even the most basic challenges women face. Their entire knowledge of women is based on a teenage girl who lived several thousand years ago and a handful of particularly pious female saints. This is why I find myself getting along a lot better with priests who have sisters; they've had some exposure to women as human beings, not as plaster statuettes representing impossible ideals.

Women can't be ordained, and it's crap. Basically, the Vatican argues that women were never ordained because there were no female apostles, but that's an intentional fallacy. There are definitely women in the New Testament who followed Jesus and who were clearly playing priestly roles in the early Church. In fact, we even know some of their names, because they're mentioned in Paul's letters and in the Acts of the Apostles and the gospel stories: sisters Mary and Martha (this Mary being the one who preferred to sit at Jesus' feet to doing the cooking and cleaning), Mary Magdalene, Jesus' mother Mary, Tabitha, Lydia, Priscia, Junia, Chloe, Julia, Euodia, Appia, Phoebe, the unnamed sister of Nereus and the unnamed wives, sisters, and daughters of Peter and all the other apostles. Even the anonymous Samaritan woman whom Jesus meets at the well is the first apostle to the Gentiles, years before Paul. Yet for a couple of thousand years we've been told that those women were servants and helpers and laundry washers and cooks and so on, but that they definitely, for sure, were not priests.

My research churns up plenty of reasons why this is probably wrong, and it also churns up another group of prayer ladies of a different sort. Back in the late 1960s when the Czech Republic and Slovakia were one country under Communist rule, the Catholic Church was forced to go underground when many priests were imprisoned and tortured for saying Mass. In order to deal with the shortage of priests, a renegade bishop ordained a woman named Ludmila Javorova, who served in the underground Catholic Church for many years and finally went public about her ordination in the mid-1990s. Javorova's ordination eventually inspired a different group of women, the Danube Seven. Back in 2002, seven women were ordained on a cruise ship floating down the Danube River. In order to claim apostolic succession— authority the Vatican believes was handed down from Jesus to Peter the first pope and to the disciples and thus to popes, cardinals, and bishops today—these women had to be ordained by a real bishop, so they found one: an Argentinean who'd been ordained in Rome before breaking off and becoming independent.

Their ordinations gave birth to what's known as the Roman Catholic Womenpriests movement, a growing group of female bishops, priests, and deacons who are running underground churches all over the world. Many of them point to the fact that the Pontifical Biblical Commission—Rome's top scholars of scripture—found in 1976 that there was *no valid case* to be made against the ordination of women based on the scriptures. Apparently, a few equality-minded male bishops agree and have been ordaining women in secret for years, thus creating a human chain leading straight from Jesus to these female priests. The Danube Seven ignored Vatican warnings and they kept on being priests, believing what the Vatican itself tells us: "Once a priest, always a priest."

It's not just the Danube Seven who embrace the idea of women's ordination. Take the case of Father Roy Bourgeois, a priest from the Maryknoll missionary order. For twenty years he worked to shut down the School of the Americas, a facility operated by the U.S. Department of Defense. Latin American military personnel were trained there, and many of them were later tried for human rights violations.

In 2008 Father Bourgeois received notice that the Vatican was excommunicating him. His grave sin? Participating in a Mass where two women were ordained, and refusing to back down on his stance that it was the right thing to do. Father Bourgeois reiterated in the *National Catholic Reporter* that there is no biblical justification for excluding women from the priesthood. "As Catholics," he wrote, "we believe that men and women are created in the image and likeness of God and that men and women are equal before God. Excluding women from the priesthood implies that men are superior to women." The Vatican Council II itself stated that "every type of discrimination . . . based on sex . . . is to be overcome and eradicated as contrary to God's intent." Surveys inform the faithful again and again that a majority of Catholics not only approve of women's ordination but would absolutely welcome it. Even brave male priests at many churches ask the congregation to pray for women's ordination, no matter what the Vatican says. Women are part of the priestly class.

Driving home after that first evening of praying and bitching, I feel buoyant about the possibility of finding a community, which is new to me—I didn't feel this way even during RCIA. The Church is too big, and often too impersonal, for anyone to navigate and understand on their own, especially someone like me who's spent a lifetime being radically minded. Whenever Catholic priests, monks, and nuns talk about taking vows in the Church, they inevitably say that it turns out obedience is harder than poverty or chastity. In the modern age, surrender of control—over your actions, over your movement, and over your beliefs—is the opposite of how we are encouraged to behave. It takes small communities, like this group of women, to understand that the real obedience required of Catholics is not to the magisterium, those cardinals and Popes who swoop through Saint Peter's square in Rome, but to something greater and more important.

A few months into spending time with the prayer ladies, I get a call from Agnes one day, who says she is hosting two Poor Clare nuns who are coming to town to guest-lecture at a college. This is odd; Poor Clares are mostly known for being cloistered, meaning they don't often leave their monasteries. (Catholic factoid: Cloistered nuns do not live in convents; they live in monasteries. Nuns who do not live in cloisters are usually called "sisters," and some of them, but not all, do live in convents.) Yet Agnes says that they are granted an exception to this rule if they have work to do and if their abbess okays it, and thus these two nuns are staying at her house for a few days. When Agnes asks if I'd like to come for dinner, there's a long moment of hesitation on my part. The only nuns in my life thus far had been the often crabby and overworked ones who ran the all-girls Catholic high school I briefly attended. The sour memories of Sister Frances, who bored us into a stupor in Religious Ed and only stopped the class to shriek at some girl (usually me), along with the pious nuns who freaked me out during the retreat, have tainted my perspective on nuns. But if the Church is ever going to make sense to me as a woman, it's probably a good idea to hear what nuns have to say for themselves outside a ninth-grade classroom, so that's how I wind up holding a bag of clementines while ringing Agnes's doorbell. I'm going to have pizza with nuns.

The Poor Clares are one of the oldest orders of women in the church, founded by Saint Clare in 1212. Saint Francis, Clare's inspiration for becoming a nun, is well known outside Catholic circles, but his basic story goes like this: born to a wealthy cloth merchant, he hears the voice of Christ telling him to "heal my church," casts off his garments in the town square and stands there naked, takes a vow of poverty, cares for lepers, preaches to birds and gets followed around by animals, forms the Franciscans, receives the stigmata, dies young.

Like Francis, Clare was born to a wealthy family in Assisi. Inspired by Francis's preaching, she ran away from home to avoid being pinned into the dull, bourgeois, often violent and oppressive marriage that was the fate of women at the time. Clare was only interested in marriage to Christ. When he saw how powerful Clare's vocation was, Francis tonsured her, cutting off her long blonde hair, and when her family witnessed this transformation, they finally gave up and let her go. Nothing like a short haircut on a woman to send the message that she doesn't care what you think. Francis and Clare had a complex relationship. Had they been less in love with God, they would likely have fallen in secular love with one another, but they veered instead toward a celibate bond, living in separate cloisters but sharing a passionate connection that lasted past Francis's death. In fact, Clare became the patron saint of television, because when Francis died, she was apparently able to see his entire funeral from within her cloister when the ceremony appeared on a wall, as if she were watching a projection screen. These two were nuts, in a good way. Francis often referred to his greatest love as "Lady Poverty," refusing to own anything, sleeping on a stone bed when indoors, wearing rags and often starving, and devoting himself to caring for the poor. Clare embraced the same ideal. They were something like spiritual twins.

Clare and her acolytes moved into San Damiano, a compound just outside the Assisi walls, which was the same crumbling church where Francis heard the voice of Christ and mistook its meaning; Francis thought he was actually supposed to get rocks and repair the building, but God wanted something bigger. At a time when the papacy was so corrupt that popes were casually keeping mistresses in the Vatican and leading armies into wars over property rights, Clare and Francis focused instead on doing what the Church now refers to as the corporal works of mercy: feeding the poor, clothing the naked, sheltering the homeless, visiting the sick and imprisoned, and burying the dead. And Clare's was the first rule of life for monastic women written by a woman. Other orders of nuns followed rules written by men.

Little of this is known to me when I walk into Agnes's kitchen and see two middle-aged women with short hair sitting around the table. My interactions with nuns had been so limited that I was only beginning to grasp the differences between contemplative and active orders, and when Agnes told me these nuns were normally cloistered, something inside me imagined them in head-to-toe habits, standing behind the grilles that separate many nuns from the people who come to visit them. (Did I imagine they had a portable grille they took with them everywhere?) But Sister Helen and Sister Veronica are wearing jeans, with large Tau crosses—Francis's symbol, a cross shaped like a *T*—swinging from chains around their necks. And my assumption that they led lives of quiet deprivation and spoke in whispers and wouldn't make eye contact with strangers was—like many assumptions I had about people in holy orders—dead wrong.

Sister Helen is the more ebullient of the two, with a face like a teenager in spite of being in her mid-seventies, and a huge smile. She has an immediately endearing habit of saying "Thanks be to GOD!" whenever somebody mentions any small good thing they've experienced, and to my surprise, she has not spent her whole life behind the grille of a monastery, but has traveled and lived all over the world. She tells us that evening about her time in Africa, where the Clares were building a foundation, and somewhere in the story she mentions getting up and "doing the Charleston for the kids in the village." She also says one of the missionary priests gave her a flare gun as protection against the pickpockets that were rife; when her purse was predictably stolen, she laughed thinking about the thief who found out that "nuns have guns," and the women around the table all fall into laughter along with her. Sister Veronica is quieter, wearing a denim shirt with the name "Joe" embroidered on the pocket, but curious about what's going on in the world in spite of the Clares' limited access to news and the Internet.

Surprising things open up over and over again. Sister Helen tells us one of the students at the college they've been visiting asked her about the knots in the cord they wear as a belt around the waists of their brown Franciscan habits. She laughs again as she recalls telling the girl, "One's chastity, one's poverty, one's . . . and then I forgot! Obedience! And she asked, 'Do you mean obedience to the Pope?'" Sister Helen smiles. "We believe in obedience to the gospel." When the girl asked about the fourth knot, Sister Helen, thousands of miles from her monastery, has to laugh again. "Oh, that's enclosure. Which I'm obviously not practicing at the moment." Sister Veronica wants to know about the speaking Agnes does in church and how people at the parish react to it. Women, we tell her, cannot wait for the days when a woman gets up to speak. It's a sign of the possibility of change. "Change is going to come from the pews," Sister Helen says, and we all nod in agreement. Women sit in church every week thinking the same thing. Another friend at the table, Bridget, who's from Ireland, tells us that there was recently a day of protest from the women of the Irish Catholic Church over the repeated revelations of sexual abuse there. Thousands of women voted with their feet and simply didn't show up one Sunday. The priests' voices must have echoed more than usual in those nearly empty churches.

Recently, the Vatican has been sending "observers" out to investigate some orders of American nuns. Many of the sisters suspect this is the beginning of a reversal of some of the freedoms they began to enjoy after Vatican II. Sisters who had left their monasteries and convents and gone out into the world dressed like everyone else were concerned they'd be forced back into habits and back behind walls, back into lives of quiet invisibility. Sisters who worked in hospitals felt like their every move was being watched for signs of moral slippage. Sisters who worked in prisons, schools, and other social justice ministries were grilled by Vatican visitors and made to feel like they were under surveillance. And yet the results of the visitations were never to be revealed to the nuns or to the public, compounding the frustrations and fear the sisters felt. The Clares, as a cloistered order, were exempt from these visitations, but that doesn't mean they lack critical opinions. They're not fond of the culture of secrecy, or the bossy, closed-minded attitude of Pope Benedict. They also long to see women at the altar. It's not that they are greedy or power-hungry, but they see women among their numbers who are called to ordination and are denied that calling.

A few weeks later, we meet again. At Agnes's kitchen table, Sister Helen passes around a copy of a painting that hangs behind the altar at Santa Chiara, the basilica of Saint Clare in Assisi. Clare is depicted standing in the middle, one hand holding a cross, the other hanging over her womb. Her face is painted in the medieval style, with a long, narrow nose and heavily hooded eyes. Running along both sides of the painting are a series of smaller images from her life, like a medieval PowerPoint: Clare runs away from home; Francis rests his hands on Clare's shoulders; the pope blesses Clare; Clare extends her hands in blessing over the body of a sick person; Clare lies down to die surrounded by her sisters. But Sister Helen calls our attention to one image in particular. In a panel on the lower right-hand side, a line of sisters is gathered behind a table with bread and wine placed on it, just like the altar during Mass. Only there's no priest blessing the bread. "Do you see what Clare's doing?" Sister Helen asks, and points at the image again. She lowers her voice to a whisper, says, "She's blessing the bread," and smiles secretively at the women around the table, letting us all in on the fact that Saint Clare, that quiet woman from Assisi who gave up everything, was given the gift of multiplication and blessing of the loaves, just like Jesus. Clare is, momentarily, a priest.

Months later, Agnes stops me after Mass and asks if I'd ever thought about getting up and delivering a gospel reflection. And I say, at that moment, no. As much as I am learning about Catholicism, I am no theologian and certainly not toeing the Vatican's line on topical issues.

But the following week, in spite of my turning her down, she introduces me as a potential speaker to the pastor, and tells him, "You need to think about the future of the church. That's Kaya here." The pastor looks me up and down, all jeans and scuffed boots and sloppy Sunday-morning hair, and chortles. "Are you trying to replace me?" he says to Agnes. But he's willing to sit down and meet with me, and after a couple of hours of conversation, I'm sent home with a stack of reading suggestions: scripture guides, a four-volume set of historical commentary called "A Marginal Jew" (that's Jesus), a lectionary with the year's Sunday readings, the names of some professors at the theology school I might want to talk to, and a date when I'm to attempt to deliver a reflection and see if I can handle it: Trinity Sunday, a few months off. When I point out the date in the lectionary, he adds that I might want to also read the whole Bible chapters for the date to help prepare, "because you need all the other shit in between to get the picture," and I know he's another guy I can trust. I mean, really—a cursing Irish priest? How could I possibly resist that?

Paging through the lectionary and then flipping open my New Jerusalem Bible so I can get "all the shit in between," I turn to the readings for Trinity Sunday, and a tingling sensation comes over my scalp. The first reading, from Proverbs, is about Wisdom, also known as Shekinah to the Jews who wrote about her and Sophia to the Gnostics who came after Christ. Yes, *her*. Wisdom, in the Proverbs' reading, is the female personification of God. I get up and dig out my copy of Sister Elizabeth Johnson's book *Quest for the Living God* (a book that was later denounced by the U.S. Conference of Catholic Bishops, to great groans of disbelief from the faithful), flip to the chapter on Wisdom, and there it is again: Wisdom is God's partner in creation, she is his "delight," his "craftperson." She plays before him in the act of creation. Something is going on in these readings that is beginning to freak me out.

Dreading what Paul, that notorious misogynist who commanded obedience for wives and recommended that women stay silent in church, will have to say on this Sunday, I flip back to the lectionary. It's from Letter to the Romans, luckily a section with nothing about women kowtowing to men. I turn to one of the Bible commentaries the pastor recommended to find out about the circumstances under which Paul wrote the letter to the Romans. Prison, persecution, et cetera . . . and then she appears. Phoebe. Paul tells the Romans the letter is being delivered by his friend Phoebe, a deacon of the church. *A deacon of the church. Don't forget: a female deacon.* It seems like Paul's sending me a little message there: don't forget that women were once leaders. Starting to feel the familiar agitation of discovery that's a little like a caffeine high, I plow through the Gospel reading, stop, read it again. Jesus is telling the disciples (among whom, we all know, were plenty of women) that God is going to send them the Spirit in his absence, that the Spirit will be the *paraclete*, the comforter. Back to the Bible commentaries. Jesus spoke to the disciples in Aramaic. In that language, and in Hebrew, and in the Syriac language that evolved from Aramaic, the word for the Spirit is feminine. Now, the idea that God is genderless, or both genders, or something beyond gender is not news to me. The main reason Catholics call him "father" is because the Latin word for God is "deus," which is masculine. And since Jesus has an earthly mother, Mary, he tends to refer to God the creator spirit as Father. But most theologians agree that there's no consensus on the real gender of God. We just don't know, and thus the best we can come up with is that God is neither male nor female but something greater than either. Yet as I'm sitting on my tattered purple couch surrounded by theology texts and Bibles all propped open to different commentaries and readings, the idea that the Spirit— the breath of God that moves through us—is referred to by Christ with a female pronoun, that Wisdom is female, that Jesus often quotes Wisdom, and that Jesus' father is not really a guy at all and that I'm being handed the opportunity to talk about all these things . . . I'm pretty sure my head is about to explode.

Rembert Weakland, who during his tenure as the archbishop of Milwaukee was admonished over and over again by the Vatican due to his support for the ordination of women, says in his memoir *A Pilgrim in a Pilgrim Church* that most Catholics are lucky if they really, truly feel the presence of God even a handful of times over the course of their lives. And this is coming from somebody who moved deep inside Vatican circles, which he found to be creepy with the worst kinds of secretive, exclusionary gossip. Yet Rome is the seat of the church, and Saint Peter's church is supposedly one of the holiest places on earth. What Archbishop Weakland's really telling us is that since God doesn't literally speak to ninety-nine point nine percent of us, we have to cling to anything resembling a sign: the conversation we have with a friend that leaves us with a feeling of being deeply and intimately understood; miraculous things in nature, like oceans and sunsets and mountains and other hippie-ish pleasures; or simply ordinary acts of grace. The problem is that most of us, myself included, are so busy and distracted and frankly annoyed by life that those signs whiz right by us and we miss almost every one.

But God is with me as I sit on my purple couch as my neighbor weed-whacks his lawn and the mailman comes by shouting into his cell phone and emails pile up unanswered. The readings, the conversations with the prayer ladies and my growing bonds with them as individuals and as a group, the volunteer work at the women's shelter, this new kind of vocational work—public speaking in a church, and the coincidence of these readings, with these revelations about faith and gender, coming at this time in my life . . . this is it. This is a sign. For once, I stop, read it, and understand.

After the Clare nuns have flown back to their monasteries, Agnes sends me a recording of the talk they gave at the college. During the Q&A, a student asks Sister Helen how she understands God. "What is God to you?" comes the voice, floating up out of my computer speakers, and I see Sister Helen's responding smile across the kitchen table again. "God is really relational energy," she replies. She goes on to explain that when Clare wrote to a fellow nun about how you should pray, Clare talked about gazing into a mirror. "Not a vanity mirror," says Sister Helen's voice, but the mirror of who you really are and how you do or don't reflect Christ. You gaze, says Clare, then you contemplate, and then you pray. And you take that energy and give it to others.

The Desert Fathers, in the earliest years of the Church, understood faith instead as a ladder: by contemplating and praying, you ascended spiritual rungs until you eventually reached Heaven. Clare, being a woman, saw it differently. Faith is internal. First you find God in yourself and working in your life, then you think about what that means, and then you go help people. That's relational energy. That's God. And that idea unlocks the whole puzzle of Trinity Sunday for me, I'm researching and writing the reflection. Deep in a book, I find a quote from the theologian Sister Sandra Schneiders that sums up what millions of women think when the Church depicts God as a dude and nothing but a dude. Schneiders is succinct in her assessment: "God," she writes, "is not two men and a bird."

That Sunday I dress up for Mass instead of pulling on my usual jeans, and within a few minutes of putting on a blazer, dress pants, and a shirt that covers all my tattoos, I am drenched in sweat. It's not just some audience in a bookstore or a classroom full of students that I'm speaking to today: God is in the house. I look around on my way into the church, and suddenly the faces I've seen every Sunday for years have meshed into one fuzzy lump. Oh, fantastic. I've forgotten my glasses.

When the gospels have been read, that beautiful passage from Proverbs slightly mangled by a dude in a Hawaiian shirt, it's finally my time to stand behind the ambo. When the ambo was first mentioned in RCIA, I had no idea what it meant, but Googling revealed that it's the Catholic name for a raised lectern, the word borrowed from the book of Isaiah, which tells the faithful that when they speak to a congregation they should "Get thee up upon a high mountain, thou that bringest good tidings to Zion: lift up thy voice with strength." *Yeah, good luck with that*, I think. My vocal cords feel like they're paralyzed, but in my damp, disheveled, half-blind state, I somehow manage to make it to the front of the church. After shuffling my wrinkled notes and gripping the ambo like a ship's rail in a storm, I lean forward into the mike.

"A couple of months ago, I was cooking eggs at the women's shelter with two other volunteers. When we began serving food, one of the guests started complaining, loudly and at length: the eggs were burnt, the coffee weak, she was getting kicked out that day. We didn't know what to say, when the volume and nature of her monologue started to change. 'My mother's got life insurance on me,' she said. 'Her life would be easier if she had the money and I was gone.' And that's when the other women staying in the shelter stepped in. They surrounded her; they gave her advice. One of them warned her about how much her mother would suffer if she did something to herself. Another suggested a place she could go for help. And their circumstances weren't any better than hers. But they worked together to help her."

"When I told this story to a friend, she looked at me and asked: 'Where do you think God was in this situation?' I'm always a bit slow in answering questions like that, but it suddenly clicked: God was in those other homeless women." I glanced up at the congregation, and could make out the fuzzy outlines of Agnes and Sage. And way in the back is my mother, who hasn't been to a Mass in years. She's brought along one of her oldest friends, another lapsed Catholic who has not walked into a church since before I was born. *Okay, lady*, I think. *Here are some people who care about you and you haven't passed out yet. Maybe you can try to keep going.*

After trying to still my shaking hands, I tell the congregation that Trinity Sunday is about understanding that God's not remote or removed or authoritative. We might find God through nature, art, or in our own idiosyncratic ways, but most of us find God in collaboration. I tell them what I learned from the Poor Clares about relational energy and finding God in other people. Paraphrasing the day's reading from Paul, I try to say something about hope having been the last thing on that homeless woman's mind when she poured out its opposites, misery and sorrow and regret, but what she found in the other women there was perhaps a little bit of hope. Just by having someone acknowledge her pain, it lessened.

Jesus repeats the word *declare* seven times in this Gospel. To declare something means to make it clear, and sometimes that can only happen when other people step in and force us to pay attention to how the Spirit is working in our lives. Otherwise, if we isolate ourselves, clarity is the last thing we feel. By this point, my hands are no longer shaking. *Go on, then.*

Ignatius asks us to meditate on the nature of the Trinity by describing them looking down on humanity: "in such variety, in dress as in actions: some white and others black; some in peace and others in war; some weeping and others laughing; some well, others ill; some being born and others dying." And that moment is when they decide to send the angel to Mary, to let her know that she will be the *theotokos*, the God-bearer. So God acts in collaboration with humans in all our turmoil, our sorrow, and in our hope. Creation is an act of compassion.

The church's music director has helped me to project a slide onto the wall during the reflection. It's a very old icon by Andrei Rubelev depicting the Trinity, but instead of showing God and Jesus sitting on gilded thrones with a dove fluttering in the background, Rubelev painted three haloed, androgynous figures sitting around a Eucharistic table. Their heads are tilted toward one another, as if they are deep in conversation. Gesturing toward it, I remind the congregation that like today's readings about Wisdom collaborating with God in creating the world, like Paul's image of his letters being carried to Rome by his friend Phoebe the deacon, the icon is a message that God cannot act alone: God needs Christ and the feminine power of the Spirit.

By now my voice has opened up. Normally it sounds thin and lispy, but maybe the microphone or the acoustics of church are working especially well today. Somehow, my voice bounces back to me, no longer strangled. "Elizabeth Johnson asks us to think of the Trinity in this way: Three notes form a chord. Or a spring comes out of the earth, and becomes a river, which in turn nourishes the ground. Or a root system, which pushes forth a stem, which in turn becomes a flower. Or simply stopping to listen to someone who is ignored, neglected, victimized, or in pain. If we can try harder to see how even the most desperate among us is willing to help someone out, then we'll see God in them." I squint at the crowd. Most Sundays, half of them are paging through the church bulletin, checking their cell phones, trying to calm down their kids. Today, though they look like a blur, something tells me they might be listening. It's like the moment I remember from playing in bands, when you hit the bridge of a song and realize that the crowd is mostly with you, that there's a collective intake of breath as you bring the beat down and finish the song.

"Hildegard von Bingen captures this living, collaborative nature of God the best. She writes that there is 'a brightness, a flashing forth, and a fire. And the three are one light in one power of potential.'"

After Mass, as I stand outside next to the priest, a stream of women comes toward me; mostly graying, primarily older, they tell me over and over that it's hard to be a woman and a Catholic. But they stay anyway.

SEVEN

SEVEN

One brilliantly sunny Sunday, Agnes, Elizabeth and I climb into Elizabeth's car. Agnes has been talking for a while now about going to visit this church in San Francisco where she delivered a talk a few weeks back. "You're not going to believe this place," she tells us as Elizabeth backs into a parking space.

The three of us climb the stairs of a large white church, and as soon as we're inside, a sweet-faced elderly man inks our names onto name tags "so that people can greet you." We climb into a packed pew in a very packed church, and it only takes a moment to realize that almost everyone around us is male. There are a couple of elderly women tottering about, all of them being embraced and kissed on the cheek, but we are definitely in the city, because the guy sitting next to me, devastatingly handsome and dressed in a perfectly tailored suit, is holding hands with another devastatingly handsome and wonderful-smelling guy. In front of us there's a row of bears, bearded and pierced; behind us are middle-aged male couples with wedding rings on their hands; there are men in dresses, men in leather, and men in stylish eyeglasses; there is a male couple across the room passing their baby back and forth; there's a man in a floral shirt and a lei; there are all kinds of men. The priest comes in and everyone stands, and the choir rains down the most sublime music I've ever heard in a Catholic church, the cantor intoning verses in a pure, high tenor. Oh my God, I think, this church is totally gay. And it's *awesome*.

The reading for today's Mass is about the woman at the well. The priest—bald, Irish, and youthful—reads Jesus' lines, a male lector reads the part of the narrator, and a female lector reads the part of the Samaritan woman, who is drawing water from a well and meets Jesus there. Back then, Jews weren't even supposed to talk to Samaritans, which is why many people equate this story with the racially segregated water fountains in the pre-civil rights era South. Jesus asks the woman for a drink, and they begin talking. With the priest and the female lector reading these parts back and forth, a new meaning begins to emerge from these verses I've heard so many times. Hearing them again, surrounded by these people who radiate affection for one another and for this place, the message of the passage is changing. When we sing the hymn "All Are Welcome" back at my home church, I always think, well, not really. According to the Vatican, gays aren't welcome, or people from other faiths, or unbelievers. But here in this church, with my friends around me, I think, *Yes*.

When Jesus asks the woman if she's married and she says no, he replies in a teasing way that she's actually been married five times, and that the man she's with now isn't her husband. "Sir," says the female lector in response, "you *must* be a prophet!" The whole congregation laughs, because it's clear what they're doing: they're flirting. This woman, like his male and female disciples, is falling in love with Christ. That's what the priest says in his homily—that Lent is a time of flirtation, when God seduces us, and Easter is when we fall in love. He adds a message I will never forget: what Jesus is showing us in this conversation with the woman at the well is a message of *radical inclusion*. And this congregation, more than any other church group I've been in, epitomizes that. Instead of sitting stupefied in the pews, they nod and laugh and sing, and after Mass, everyone files downstairs for coffee, and I run into a transvestite in the women's bathroom, whom I compliment on her 1940s hat.

Afterward at brunch, as we're eating and marveling at that being one of the best liturgies any of us has ever attended (and Agnes and Elizabeth, being in their sixties, have attended *a lot* of liturgies), a middle-aged male couple keeps waving us over. They remember Agnes from the time she spoke there, and they ask how we liked the Mass. "Amazing," I say. "It's just amazing." One of them smiles and takes my hand. "You know," he says with a wink, "it's the best happy hour in town."

✳

Gay people were welcomed into my Catholic home: one of my sisters' best friends in college, a gay man, babysat my younger sister and me on occasion and we adored him. I've played backup cello for a transgendered Nico impersonator, campaigned for a drag queen friend running for public office, sat with gay and lesbian students of mine as they agonized over coming out, and have stood on the sidelines at the Pride parade for many, many years waving at friends. God chose to make me a straight person, but all evidence indicates that gender and sexuality are fluid. I won't pull a Lady Gaga and say that I speak on behalf of gay Catholics or that they require a spokesperson when they are perfectly capable of speaking for themselves. What matters is that like a rather large proportion of straight Catholics, I think gay people are pretty much the same as everyone else. My belief about sexuality can be summed up in this way: no matter our sexual orientation, we are all acts of divine creation and beloved by God.

The Church, of course, does not feel the same. The best it can come up with is John Paul II's nauseating declaration that we should "love the sinner, hate the sin." And the official doctrine, that homosexuality is "objectively disordered" (i.e., contrary to nature), not only fails to make logical sense in light of evolutionary indications that same-sex attraction exists across many species and not just in humans, but also runs against the findings of the American Psychological Association, which removed homosexuality from its list of diagnoses all the way back in 1973. A friend of mine said that her problem with Catholicism was it being "so medieval," and it's true that the Church's antiquated and homophobic views of gay sexuality epitomize that notion.

Yet the more time I spend in the Church, and the more Catholics I get to know, the more of them turn out to be openly gay, in the closet but with the door cracked, or at the very least straight but completely supportive of total social equality. And that group of people includes many priests and nuns. One night during pray-and-bitch group, Elizabeth begins talking about a friend of hers who's a priest, and how excited he is to wear his hot pink vestments for Passion Sunday. "And, well, he's gay," she says. And Margaret, gay herself, laughs and says, "Well, how many of them aren't?" And Elizabeth laughs too and says, "If I had a nickel for every gay priest . . ." And after we giggle we decide that if every gay priest, nun, bishop, cardinal, and pope came out of the closet on the same Sunday, the Church would probably explode from the collective force of all those closet doors being blown open.

The number of LGB and even T male and female clerics is impossible to pin down, given the culture of closeting and secrecy they're stuck with, but suffice to say that it's been sussed out by the laity that there are more than a few gay and lesbian people in the clergy. In the past, if your sexuality was forbidden to be expressed publicly and you had some sort of religious calling, being in holy orders offered you a community and a way to channel your sexual feelings into something else. Of course, celibacy is painful, lonely, and difficult for people of any sexual orientation, and thus the rate of attrition for gay and lesbian clerics is just as high as it's always been for straight ones. Yet some of these holy men and women were comfortable enough to talk privately about their feelings with friends and flock, and therefore it became a kind of open secret in Catholicism. However, it's the kind of secret that costs a lot of people their happiness and psychological well-being. The writer Dan Savage told a story on NPR about his very Catholic mother's reaction to his coming out. She ran to her priest, who knew her son as well, and when she told the priest how distressed she was about her son's sexuality, he told her he was gay too. "And it's better for Dan that he's out," the priest said, patting her knee.

Homophobia has a long, complicated social history and I'm no sociologist, but many of the roots of homophobia in the church can be traced to mistranslations and misinterpretations of biblical language. Tinkering around with search strings, I'm able to find several books in the library that break down the primary biblical passages historically used to argue that homosexuality is contrary to nature. The first one, from the Old Testament book Leviticus, states that same-sex activity is "an abomination," yet the Hebrew word *toevah*, which got translated as "abomination," doesn't mean the act is intrinsically evil; rather, it refers to something ritually unclean like breaking the Jewish dietary laws just before going to temple. Jewish laws are mind-bogglingly complex and often difficult to understand from a contemporary point of view (No mixed fibers? No shellfish? No cutting your beard's "corners"?) and thus it's likely that the author of Leviticus is not necessarily condemning homosexuality, just the timing of a few homosexual acts.

The only other place in the Bible where homosexual acts are explicitly mentioned in a negative light is in Paul's letters to the Corinthians and Timothy, which, according to a few theologians, have been taken to mean gay people will not inherit the kingdom of heaven—but, interestingly, the interpretation's only been popular since the beginning of the twentieth century, around the time that homosexuality began to become more of an open topic. Praise be to Saint Oscar Wilde for being brave about that. One of Paul's words translated as "homosexual" is actually the Greek word meaning "soft," which is not really a bad thing to be. But as gay people began to be more public about their love for one another, religious leaders didn't bother to look up the Greek definition and started throwing those passages from Paul around like weapons. As we've seen way too many times throughout history, the meaning of the Bible can be twisted and manipulated by anyone with an agenda. When faced with this sort of distortion, it's helpful to recall that there are seven lines in the entire Bible about homosexuality, whereas there are hundreds, maybe thousands, about caring for the poor and outcast. Perspective is key.

As to what Jesus says about homosexuality, the answer is . . . nothing. Absolutely nothing. The only thing Jesus explicitly forbids in relationships is divorce, but even in that context, he is not referring to the same sort of divorce we have today, but to Talmudic law. And under that law, a man can divorce his wife for any reason and without her consent, so Jesus is actually being a bit of a sneaky feminist in condemning that act. As far as what Jesus thought about gay people, or whether he hung out with them, or even whether he was one himself, we'll never know. We do know that he read Torah, which includes depictions of close, loving relationships between Ruth and Naomi, David and Jonathan, and Daniel and Ashpenaz. We also know whom Jesus kept company with, and those people typically included the most marginal populations in his society. If Jesus were alive today, would he hang out with gay people? Well, let's see. They are frequently persecuted. Check. They are often scored and judged. Check, check. And because of this oppression, they are therefore beloved by God. Checkity check check.

The problem is that the culture of homophobia is so entrenched in the upper echelons of the Church that it is nearly impossible to believe that any of the people condemning acts of love have actually bothered to read the parts of the Bible that talk about loving one another. Their focus on Leviticus and that quote from Paul make it seem like they're literalists when it comes to scripture. However, despite what many of my atheist friends believe, Catholics are not fundamentalists. I have never heard a Catholic say that the earth is 6,000 years old; in fact, at the Christmas midnight Mass, the proclamation that's sung at the beginning says the world began "unknown ages from the time when God created the heavens and earth." I like to call this the "suck it, creationists" portion of the evening. In spite of the Galileo debacle,

Catholicism has done a pretty good job of embracing science and evolution in recent times. And both Vatican II and the catechism encourage us to read scriptures not as literal facts but as forms of divinely inspired creative writing, open to interpretation and subject to historical context. But even with scientific and psychological evidence that people are born with innate same-sex attraction, conservative Catholics will haul out Leviticus and those mistranslated lines from Paul all over again.

The fact of the matter is that Catholicism is terrible at dealing with sex in any way, shape, or form. The disgusting legacy of priestly abuse is part of that; so is the equally disgusting legacy of conservatives blaming that abuse on gay priests. The John Jay commission's 2011 report on abuse (a Vatican-sponsored legal examination that blames sex abuse on the 1960s counterculture) revealed that when more gay men entered the priesthood in the 1980s, the number of abuse cases *decreased*. I have friends who were victims of priest abuse, and I understand why they left the Church or want to burn down the Vatican. Every person involved in that abuse and those who participated in the cover-up, from the Vatican on down, should be in jail, period. But the conflation of the abuse scandal with the rise in a social acceptance of homosexuality makes no sense. Pedophilia and homosexuality are not the same thing. Like the Church's pushback against women, this conflation further alienates a huge group of Catholics who could work miracles of meaningful reform if they were allowed a voice.

At Saint Sebastian's church in the city, what I saw being enacted was exactly the message Jesus sends the woman at the well: radical inclusion. Historically marginalized people coming together in community to celebrate their love of God and of one another. No doubt, there are gay Catholics at pretty much every parish in the world, but even at my own relatively progressive parish, gay people are not the majority in the pews. So the fact that churches like Saint Sebastian's even exist is not only anomalous, but startling. Somehow, these men and women have found a way to reconcile their sexuality with a Church that condemns it. Discovering how that happened, finding out that there is a large and growing movement within lay Catholicism for greater equality for LGBT people, and understanding why this matters right now more than ever before in the history of Catholicism, turns out to be a turning point in my own experience with faith. It's also the prelude to my first real experience of the wrath of the right-wing nutjob side of the Church.

Back in the 1970s, a Sister of Notre Dame named Jeannine Gramick befriended a gay man while she was studying for a PhD, and she subsequently became involved in providing pastoral ministry to LGBT people who had become alienated from the Catholic Church. Along with Father Robert Nugent, she cofounded the group New Ways Ministry, and for more than twenty years Sister Gramick traveled all over the country doing ministerial work to help LGBT Catholics with the hard work of squaring their consciences with the Church's homophobia.

The main idea espoused by New Ways was reconciliation: the group not only reached out to LGBT Catholics but also reached out to bishops and priests in order to attempt to open their minds about the LGBT people in their congregations. In 2000, Sister Gramick was informed that the Vatican's Congregation for the Doctrine of the Faith, then led by Cardinal Ratzinger (yep, later Pope Benedict), had censured her work and that she was effectively prohibited not only from ministering to the LGBT community but also from writing about it, speaking about it, or even speaking or writing about the censure. But rather than capitulating to the Vatican's message that she needed to send a message that homosexuality was intrinsically disordered, Sister Gramick kept up her ministry. When her order threatened to cast her out, she joined a more sympathetic order, the Sisters of Loretto, and continued her work.

A few years before New Ways was formed, an Augustinian priest named Patrick Nidorf also began ministering to gays and lesbians in Los Angeles. Within a year, the group he founded, Dignity, was growing quickly enough to advertise in *The Advocate*, and it grew steadily throughout the 1970s and 1980s. Nidorf left the Augustinians, and the organization has subsequently been run by laypeople, but it does have the support of a few brave clerics. Dignity's emphasis is less on reconciliation with the Vatican and more on an Act Up-style, in-your-face ministry of agitation. On Dignity's website, you can find photos of people marching to diocesan offices when bishops were quoted saying something homophobic, picketing in front of churches with homophobic priests, and, in my favorite photo, nailing a letter of protest to the door of the Vatican's Congregation for the Doctrine of the Faith (formerly known as the Office of the Roman Inquisition . . . oh, dear). Forbidden from meeting in Catholic churches by bishops, Dignity holds services in Protestant churches and has organizing groups sprinkled across the United States.

I first heard about Sister Gramick's mission from my friend Margaret, who can perhaps best be described as "intense," and who was intensely pissed about Sister Gramick's Vatican censure. Margaret told me that when she came out in her thirties, she'd expected her fellow Catholics to reject her or push her away, when in fact they did the opposite. While she worried she'd lose what she calls "her church," eventually, she found a place where she could be fully herself. But that doesn't mean she complacently accepts any transmission of ideas about what gay people should or shouldn't be; rather, she openly disagrees, and we talk about it and try to figure out what we can do other than walking out of the Church forever.

Back at my home church, I ask Father Mellow about a woman I see every week. I'd spotted her wearing a Soulforce T-shirt, which stopped me in my tracks: I'd just donated some money to Soulforce, a nonprofit that agitates for equality for LGBT people in especially conservative Christian denominations, including the Catholic Church. "Oh, that's Joan," Father Mellow says. "She left the church for a long time and got into Wicca. Then she came out. And then she came back to the Church." Telling this story, he's totally nonchalant, as if ex-Wiccan lesbians just happened to wander into his church every day. But when it's time for communion, I get in line to receive from her. And I chase her down after Mass and we talk. As I expected, she's a fireball: she protested against Proposition 8 (California's ban on same-sex marriage) in front of the local cathedral, writes newsletters for a Catholic group lobbying for gay marriage, and heads up the parish social justice group.

One day, I get an email from her. She's copied this to a ton of people from our church, and reading it, I can tell she's clearly upset. Apparently, our church has sponsored a speaker at a nearby venue who's openly ranted against gays. He's a priest who's been quoted comparing gay marriage to bestiality. "I feel betrayed by my church," she writes, and the links to this priest's website are stomach-turning and vile. And then, as emails go around and we try to figure out how this guy wound up being asked to speak, the story gets weird: as it turns out, the speaker wasn't actually invited by our church, but was asked to come by a parishioner who's friends with the local bishop, who is himself an appointed member of the Vatican's anti-gay marriage squadron in the United States. Joan's righteous indignation leads to a barrage of emails from parishioners to the pastor, and soon all the flyers are pulled down, the announcements disappear from the bulletin, a group of anti-homophobia people turn up at the speaker's event to protest, one of our priests delivers a fantastic homily in support of LGBT Catholics, and an LGBT group is formed at the church for young people, the very target audience for the talk. It all happens so fast it's like whiplash. But it reminds me that when we work together, radical Catholics really can work for change.

Five months after my Trinity reflection, I get invited to deliver a reflection at Saint Sebastian's. Every year, it has Vespers services for Lent and Advent, and with Advent coming up they're looking for speakers and a friend has recommended me. I write the church back quickly, telling them I'm a huge fan and would be more than happy to help out.

Preparing for a reflection is kind of like being back in graduate school: pen between my teeth, notebook open, trying to puzzle out a two-thousand-year-old text and to decide how to relate it to something happening today, with a much smarter person like Agnes nudging me along, followed by hours and hours of more work on my own. While I can knock off an essay in a couple of days if I'm really revving my engines, church reflections take weeks, coming one line at a time if I'm lucky. The job of breaking open the gospel means not only translating it and explaining what it theoretically might mean, but also explaining to a diverse—and often bored and disinterested—audience why, exactly, it matters today.

This gets even tougher when said reflection is delivered at a church I don't regularly attend, so I decide to learn more about the history of Saint Sebastian. And this becomes ridiculously easy when my neighborhood bookstore—which happens to be run by an incredibly sweet and knowledgeable former priest—turns out to have a copy of a book about the very same church, written by the very same Irish priest who delivered that amazing homily about the woman at the well. Like a lot of neighborhoods in the Bay Area, the part of the city where the church is located started changing in the 1960s. It was historically populated by working-class Irish, and the city church catered to them for decades. But when gay men originally started to gravitate to the neighborhood, it posed an obvious challenge for the aging population of the area, who were bewildered by the sudden arrival of thousands of hairy gay men. (Remember, it was the 1960s. Everyone was hairy.) As the Irish population began aging and dying off, the pews in the city church got emptier and emptier. By the 1970s and 1980s, it was dying.

The pastor who arrived in the 1980s took a leap of faith and invited the gay community to events at the church. Slowly, in small numbers at first, these men who'd been told for decades that they were sinners came back to the church. And the parishioners who welcomed them were mainly old ladies. As their more conservative husbands died off, these elderly women embraced the men who had often been rejected or abandoned by their own families. It was a unique, even bizarre vision of community, but it worked: the church began to grow. Bonds were forged between the elderly women and the younger men, and the younger men began inviting their friends. When AIDS arrived and ravaged the community in horrifying numbers, the church opened a hospice, held vigil Masses, and offered support to caretakers and victims alike.

Reading this story reminds me of the real meaning of the word *catholic*: all-encompassing. If a dying church full of elderly people can adapt and grow along with an unexpected new community, in theory, the same thing could happen to the big *C* Church as well. But Saint Sebastian is constantly under fire, both from blowhard conservatives and even from non-religious types who graffitied its walls with anti-Catholic hate messages when Proposition 8 was passed (never mind the fact that most of the parishioners voted no on 8). By taking what seems like a logical step and embracing the community surrounding it, Saint Sebastian has become damned if you do, and damned if you don't. The world has changed in recent decades, and it has mostly changed for the better when we're talking about LGBT people from a social justice point of view. So any church that telegraphs the message that God loves you as you are because God made you as you are should be lauded, not condemned. Doesn't Jesus tell us that every hair on our heads has been counted, not that he's going to burn them all off?

One December morning as I'm drinking coffee and checking my email for grouchy student complaints about final grades, a Google alert arrives in my inbox. This was set up on the advice of my former book publicist and has caused me nothing but agony, because every shitty blog comment or crappy book review or inane Twitter post complaining about my writing arrives like a brick through a window. But some part of me must be drawn toward martyrdom, because I've never turned it off. I open the email link to find something very disturbing.

Saint Sebastian has a website, and they post announcements of upcoming events there all the time. Nobody would even notice these updates unless they were interested, and, as it turns out, many people are. Most of them are parishioners and friends of the church. A few, however, include some very right-wing Catholic bloggers, including a website that seems to have exhaustively chronicled any "liberal" move made by a church in California for the past decade or so. And Saint Sebastian, unsurprisingly, is one of its favorite targets. An article about the service where I'll be speaking claims that the agenda of all the talks is "approval of homosexuality" (that's news to me: the liturgy director told me it was about Advent), and that all the speakers—myself included—are proponents of gay marriage. They must have found this out by doing a Google search and discovering that my profile on a social networking site has a "Repeal Prop 8" badge. That's awfully lazy research, because if they'd dug deeper they'd have found the article I wrote about my intense distaste for Pope Benedict, or photos of me playing music with my transwoman friend. Maybe the fact that I teach at Berkeley was enough to give me away.

The article is gross enough, but worse still are the comments. "I could easily say that I approve of homosexuality," one anonymous person chimes in, "adding that I also approve of dwarves, mental retardation, and cerebral palsy." "It's difficult to imagine Satan himself doing a more destructive job than the pastor of this church," adds another. "Being gay is a choice. Sin is a choice," blurts another. "The word *homosexuality* was coined by this aberrant community to replace the less delectable label of *sodomite*," adds a particularly long-winded commenter, who also disapproves of my using the form "Ms.," because that's "another small thing to ruin the traditional roles of men and women, and the feminists' and Communists' answer to equality."

By the time I get down to the bottom of the comments page, my gorge is rising. The coffee has gone cold and my palms are leaking sweat. And a few more clicks reveal the article has been picked up by other conservative bloggers. One particularly virulent woman calls the other speakers "flamers," rants about a priest friend of hers who only wanted to go back to the Latin Mass and molested a few kids along the way but, hey, we should forgive him but never the gays, and then she hauls out her big axe. All liberal Catholics, she writes, "are HERETICS."

This heretic is by now shaking with anger. I'm not pissed because some loon finally pinned the heretic label on me—that was bound to happen sooner or later, and it'll make a great bumper sticker someday—I'm pissed because there is so much hatred and bile directed at these people who have done nothing wrong. For decades, they have fed the hungry, ministered to the sick, housed the homeless and made a place for anyone who wanted to come in. And these Internet commenters, hiding behind anonymous screens, are condemning them to burn in Hell.

By the time Sage wakes up an hour later, he finds me curled up in a damp angry ball. I show him my laptop screen. "Fuckers," he says after a minute, and begins pecking away at the keyboard. Soon enough, he discovers that the editor of the newsletter is a notorious California conservative lobbyist. And this conservative is rich, which means he has money to throw at whatever cause he wants. He's usually agitating for a return to the Latin Mass, head coverings on women, all kneeling all the time, and a repeal of Vatican II. His favorite targets are gay people, single women or those who don't have kids, Planned Parenthood, any religious order that dares to be even slightly liberal, and any parish that opens its doors to any of those groups.

Homophobia exists, and it's ugly, and to be honest, I've never seen it up close before. Many of my friends who came to live in the Bay Area came fleeing exactly this kind of attitude, but in all my days and nights with them, I've never confronted this kind of talk. The Bay Area is the kind of place where same-sex couples can walk openly holding hands and transvestites step out in broad daylight. Living in this bubble of progress makes witnessing this kind of bullshit even more disturbing. Sage talks me down by reminding me that gay people deal with this stuff far more often than he or I do:

"They have to grow a thick skin," he says, and he's right. It's not fair, but it's true—any member of a minority has to deal with way more shit than I ever will as a white, straight woman.

But it still hurts to see this hate, and it hurts because, ultimately, faith is a love story. Over and over, Christ tells us to love one another, love our enemies, love the people who persecute us. The Catholic Church is so good at ministering to the poor, caring for the sick, educating people in forgotten communities. It is so good at encouraging its flock to stand up to injustice and fight oppression. And it is just freaking awful at understanding what it means to be a woman, or to be gay, or to want to express your sexuality without catching a disease. Yet what being Catholic has given me is a sense of love and compassion for the people around me that was pretty much absent in my decades of fake atheist faithlessness.

Hatred is the opposite of Christ's message. It is the opposite of what I witness at the women's shelter, at pray and bitch, while reading the gospels, while talking to the priests and nuns who reassure me there is a place in this church for someone like me. It is the opposite of the calls for peace and justice I hear in church every week. In every case when I've raised an objection about my worthiness to believe—that I am damned or sinful—I have not been met with judgment, but with compassion and love. And in spite of my generational propensity for snark and cynicism, being Catholic has taught me to give compassion and love in return.

So that's what I plan to bring to Saint Sebastian for my

reflection. Early mornings, I've been at my desk basking in the light from a lamp that's supposedly going to lift my seasonal affective disorder. That's the time when I read scripture. And for this Advent talk, I've been reading what little there is to be found out about Joseph, the foster-father of Jesus, as he's the main operator in the reading about the flight into Egypt, the topic for my talk. Joseph is one of the most obscure figures in the New Testament. He only appears a handful of times, and he never speaks. Not a word. Having grown up with a father who never stopped speaking, this concept of a silent father amuses me. We can't know for sure that Joseph was really a carpenter; the Greek word *tekton*, used to describe his occupation, is actually more of a catch-all for anybody who builds.

But I keep coming back to the fact that Joseph never speaks. Every time he's depicted, he has to listen to some message and act on it, but he never says anything: never protests, or shakes his fist, Job-like, at God, never rolls his eyes or fakes coughs as I do whenever someone says something narrow-minded in church. Maybe reading all these conservative Catholic rants is teaching me that instead of sitting at home giving the finger to my laptop screen, I should listen and go out into the world and respond in a rational fashion. Maybe reason and love will eventually trump irrational hate. Oftentimes it's damn hard to hear what God wants. After all, God's not exactly chattering away with any of us, least of all me. But the gospel reminds me again and again that I really need to turn down the mental chatter. Just listen, it says. Just try.

✳

When Sage and I board the late afternoon train in Oakland, it's still light outside, murky pink and gray light hovering over Telegraph Avenue. By the time we arrive in San Francisco it's already dark, and as we walk up a long sloping hill toward Saint Sebastian's, part of me worries about all those conservative bloggers. What if some of them show up bearing torches, threatening to burn the gay-loving heretic writer at the stake? Maybe this image has been playing through my mind a little bit too often in the past few weeks. I've just cut my hair so short my scalp shows through, and tonight I've worn boots that lace up to the knee. It's my Joan of Arc look. I'm trying to bring some love and listening to the table, but just in case I have to defend myself from Internet loonies, a warrior outfit can't hurt.

A handful of people are seated in the pews, mostly middle-aged guys and a couple of elderly ladies, the same crowd I saw here before. Among them are my friend Judith and her mother Ruth, who, like so many of my friends, are Jewish. When Judith was a kid, they went to a progressive synagogue where members of the congregation gave the reflections every week and folk music was played during services. A few weeks before, I'd told Judith I was delivering a reflection at a Catholic church and then described Saint Sebastian's, and she laughed. "That sounds very familiar," she said. Judith is bi, and her mother is a fierce supporter of gay rights, and both she and Judith's late father believed in an open-minded version of their faith. So Judith and I may have been raised in different religions, but our childhood modes of worship were very similar. Neither Judith nor Ruth have been in a Catholic church before, but when I go to hug them, they both smile. "We were trying to sit in the back," Judith says, "but the usher moved us up front." "That's fine," Ruth added. "But I told him there's no way we're making the sign of the cross." "Please don't!" I reply, laughing. "No one will mind." And I head off to introduce myself to the priest.

Along the way, one of the guys in the pews stops me and hands me a sheaf of papers. "These are for you," he says with a smile. I glance down and see what looks like Greek lettering. "It's a translation of tonight's readings by a friend of mine," he explains, and I flip the pages. "She's trying to re-translate the Gospels into gender-neutral language and I'm helping her out." I smile and give him a big thanks and a handshake. He leans closer to me, conspiratorial. "My friend's one of those Catholic Womenpriests," he says. And I beam at him. God likes to surprise me like this. "I hope I get to meet her someday," I say. I've only met a female Catholic priest once before, in the middle of a massive protest over budget cuts on the Berkeley campus. She was talking to a couple of my colleagues as we stood under the shade of a tree. When she walked up wearing clericals and a Roman collar, with a big straw hat tipped behind her tiny shoulders, I was naturally curious about her. So when my colleagues introduced us, I asked her if she was an Episcopalian priest. She chortled. "Nope! I'm a Catholic priest." And she was on her way to preach at a Dignity Mass. Out of the ten thousand people at the protest that day, the one I wound up standing next to turned out to be a female Catholic priest who ministers to the LGBT community.

I like the priest at Saint Sebastian's immediately. He's affable and funny—and also wearing very swanky, Christmassy vestments, gold with green trim. I ask what he's got planned for Christmas, and he says, "Chinese food and Netflix. Everyone in the congregation wants me to come over, and it's sweet, but I really need a night off." After almost high-fiving him for being a fellow introvert, I agree that it sounds like my dream Christmas too. We head out into the hallway so we can make a procession back into the church, and while we're waiting for the music to start I notice his sleeve fall back a little and lo and behold: he's got a tattoo on his inner arm.

Back in a pew next to Sage, the music continues and the cantor begins to intone chants. Sage nods toward the singer and says, "Nice." One of his chief complaints about my regular church is the weekly repetition of sincerely sung but frequently off-key Catholic folk rock tunes the choir specializes in. The Catholic Mass is beautiful, all those words and gestures and rituals entwining into something hard to resist, but cheese is cheese when it comes to music. Even though I've mostly abandoned playing in bands, I still cringe when a choir member hits a sour note and it spreads through the whole congregation.

But Saint Sebastian's really does up the liturgy. There's a ton of incense, that amazing singing, candles everywhere, flowers and Christmas trees and gilding and lights. It really feels like a space where God would be happy to kick back and hang out. Who cares about these people's sexual orientation? What does it have to do with the way they use this space to show how much they love God? Those bloggers have it all wrong. If they could only see that male couple lovingly tending to their four (four!) kids, if they could see the way the whole church looks at those kids like they're the best kids in the entire world, if they could see how these men love these old ladies and how these old ladies love these men, if they could witness the work they've done for people dying from AIDS, if they could watch them feeding the homeless . . . maybe they'd re-think their idea that God's turned his back on this congregation. Maybe they'd remember that Jesus tells us the greatest commandments are to love God, and one another. Not to judge.

A white-haired woman in a spangled holiday sweater delivers the readings, more chants are sung, and then it's time for me to stand at the ambo. I look out at the congregation, these people beloved by God, and take a breath.

"Advent encourages us to tend to the things deep inside ourselves. Those of you heading to a midnight Mass in a few days will hear Isaiah's words: 'The people who walked in darkness have seen a great light; upon those who dwelt in the land of gloom a light has shone.'"

Winter has always been a time of struggle for me. Depression peaks and churns with the absence of light. I loathe waking in the dark, stumbling through the house with my hands flung out like a spastic dancer. Driving home from a day of teaching while watching the sun go down before 5 PM feels like witnessing the end of the world. Catholicism has helped me redefine this season to an extent. Yes, I still spend dark mornings brooding over my coffee and willing the sun to just fucking rise already, but I also understand it's a season of waiting, of anticipation, of turning toward a new kind of light.

That repetition throughout the liturgies of the season of this theme, the anticipation of light, the meaning of light, the Son coming as light from light, forms a rhythm inside my consciousness. The O Antiphons of Advent—the evening prayers sung at Vespers for thousands of years—each night reveal one of the seven names of Christ, and they culminate on December 23rd with the one that matters most: Emmanuel, God-with-us. I've been listening to the Antiphons in these evenings before Christmas, called the Golden Nights in the medieval church, learning these names for God: O Wisdom, O Lord, O Root of Jesse, O Key of David, O Dayspring, O King of Nations, O God with Us. It makes the sight of the bug-eyed plastic rooftop reindeer on my neighbor's house almost bearable.

Matthew 2:13-23 tells the story of the Holy Family's exile: as soon as Jesus was born, he was chased out of Israel. As I prepared for tonight, I thought of all my friends who'd fled home places where they were told they were freaks. Living in the Bay Area, they found refuge.

The reading also touches on another exile: the beginning

of what many theologians refer to as the "hidden life" of Christ; the years when he evolves as a man, out of sight of the world. Those years are a mystery that drives lots of people nuts: What did he do? Where did he go? Who was this God-man becoming? Squinting against the spotlight trained on the ambo, I tell the congregation that the story teaches us to reframe the idea of exile, helping us to imagine it not as a time of isolation, but as a time of formation.

The environment in Israel during the time of Jesus' exile "would be called a police-state, complete with loyalty oaths, surveillance, informers, secret police, imprisonment, torture and brutal retaliation against any serious dissenter," writes professor and author Richard Horsely. The Holy Family fled Israel because of those conditions, a story that could just as easily apply to millions of people today. I quote activist theologian Ched Myers—"the savior of the world begins life as a political refugee"—and get a smile from the guy playing the piano. Later, he'll tell me that his parents were refugees from Eastern Europe, and they starved for years as they made a new life in the States. I recall some of the women I've served at the shelter, the ones who come from Mexico and Central America, straining to start a new life, and even some of my students, here in the States illegally, or with parents being threatened with deportation. This old story of a family fleeing oppression is one that never ends.

But I've learned that it's in exile that we sometimes find a home. That is certainly true for me. Once I found my way back to the Church—even though the journey is continuous—I was exiled for good from the world of atheism. I was exiled forever from engaging in conversations with friends who bashed religion again and again. *Let them rant*, I think when they get started. Sometimes I bash religion too. *Let them keep bashing*, I say as I scroll through my Facebook feed, article after article about the evil pope, child-molesting priests, unfairly treated nuns. I rant against those forces too. And even if they are still bewildered by the things I believe, a few people from my pre-Catholic years have come with me on the journey, unbelievers willing to trust that I don't think they are going to Hell. That includes my husband, who's giving me a nod of confidence from his pew. When I occasionally manage to bring him to Mass back at my home church, Father Mellow always shakes his hand, nods toward me, and says, "He's your biggest fan." I love that cheesy sentiment because, after all these years and after all the things Sage and I have been through, it is mostly true. He may not be my biggest fan when I'm stomping around the house in high heels at 6:00 AM while he's fast asleep, or when I'm snarling about writing that's not going well, but even though he's not Catholic, he's forgiving.

Standing before this small, strange congregation, I understand that we are all the Holy Family now. Unbelievers may complain that Christians run everything, but Catholics—especially gay Catholics and the straight Catholics who love them—are not exactly steering the ship. We've exiled ourselves from the mainstream of the Church. So this church, full of exiles, is now my home too. These days, I laugh harder than my unbelieving friends at Catholic jokes, because the joke is on me, and I like it. And I like some churches more than others. At the ones where priests are cruel or the congregation is terrified of change, I know I don't belong—and I feel pain for Catholics who think they do belong there. When a priest spouts homophobia or crushes the idea of female independence in his homily, I know there are better things out there—better churches, better priests, better ways of believing. And I get up, walk out, and never return.

Joseph, the human father of Jesus, remains a puzzle throughout most of the Gospels, and this section in Matthew is one of the few that tells us anything about him. When I'd gone to Vespers at Saint Sebastian the previous week, the readings reminded me of Joseph's righteousness: how he kept his promise to Mary in spite of what was essentially an out-of-wedlock pregnancy; how he raised Jesus in a traditional Jewish home, reading Torah together, going to temple, honoring the Jewish laws. I thought of my own father, staying with us even when he wanted to walk away, ushering us into churches, letting us know about God. Above my desk there's a picture of him, sitting next to my godfather just after my baptism. I'm a pale wrinkle in a white gown. My godfather's just come from working with refugees in Africa and is wearing a dashiki and oversized 1960s eyeglasses as he holds me in his arms. And my father, squinting from the flash, is managing that rarest of things he showed us: a kind of lopsided smile.

Another thing about Joseph: his silence. Exile is a kind of enforced silence, since immigrants and anyone fleeing oppression don't have much of a voice, but Joseph is literally silent: we never hear a thing he says. So a lot of theologians talk about Joseph's life as a "hidden life," like those mystery years between Jesus' birth and the beginning of his public ministry. But a hidden life can still be significant. Joseph's silence speaks multitudes. He knows how to listen. During days like this when darkness is pressing in, listening can be the hardest thing of all.

The air's filled with the resin of Frankincense, pine drifting over from the spangled tree, sulphur left over from matches used to light candles, some note of the congregation's blended colognes underneath all of it. And all of us breathe in this Advent smell, together. "Silence and exile force all of us to slow down, to be more patient, and to be more aware of the people around us, especially those whose own lives are hidden," I say. "Listening is a challenge for many of us in the Catholic Church today. For people in the LGBT community, for women, for anyone who feels marginalized or misunderstood, we have to listen harder in order to find representation and resonance. But, as they did for Joseph, the messages of what we should do will come to us at unexpected times." The more I interact with other Catholics, the more I learn about how many of us are working for a more inclusive and welcoming church, even in small ways that remain hidden to people on the outside. My pray-and-bitch friends, the priests who have helped me, the nuns who surprise me with their radical opinions are all with me as I look out at this congregation.

When I glance down at my notes again, I find them curling at the edges, and press those edges down with my palms. "As adults, we seek communities of like-minded people. We find our families of choice. If the adult Christ found his own family of choice among the most despised and marginalized people in his society, to me that means that many of us, whether we grew up here or arrived seeking a tolerant community, should feel even more of a kinship with him. We love one another more for being outcasts, and accompany one another. We are lights to one another."

EIGHT

Guido de Pietro was a good church guy. Born in a small Tuscan town late in the fourteenth century, he joined the Carmelite order and was rechristened Fra Angelico, or "Brother Angel." In surviving portraits, he has the same high-bridged nose and hooded eyes of the Italian men jostling and shoving their way around Sage and me in the Uffizi gallery, packed this morning with shuffling hordes. But Sage and I are holding our ground, standing in front of a modest, muddy painting. Among all the gilded church art that crams the Uffizi walls, it's a smudgy, mostly gray landscape of undulating Italian hills that look so suspiciously like Marin County in the Bay Area that when I see them, I wonder if we really left home. On the painted hills there are dozens of tiny huts, and poking out the window of each is the head of a bearded Catholic hermit. Many of them are depicted giving holy advice to penitents, who are offering the hermits hunks of cheese and pieces of fruit in return. One of the hermits appears to be sharing his dinner with a large black dog. Others are simply rolling their eyes toward Heaven.

When we began planning this trip and it turned out that we'd arrive in Italy on New Year's Eve, it made sense to go straight to Florence, city of Dante and major historical debauchery. From here we'll head to Rome, where, in theory, holiness and hedonism will merge, and then to Assisi, home of Francis and Clare. In this manner, I may be attempting to shape this trip around my own journey into a Catholic life: from a secular obsession with radical creativity to flashes of holiness to a sustained attempt to mingle the two.

We landed just a few days after my talk at Saint Sebastian's, stumbled through Fiumicino airport, with its bewildering emergency exit signs depicting a stick man running straight into a wall; pushed through the crowds at Rome's Termini Station; and boarded a fast train marked FIRENZE.

The Uffizi is a claustrophobic clusterfuck: jam-packed with vacationing Italians in shiny puffy coats, tour groups wearing matching hats; metal detectors operated by security guards who have a habit of wandering off to smoke, leaving dozens of people waiting in line; our fellow Americans being noisy and dumb; and all that Medici loot shoved into what feels like an endless series of teeny, tiny rooms, like a very fancy ant farm. Even the upstairs patio provides little respite, as it too is packed with people snapping cell phone photos of one another in front of the astonishing view of the Arno.

Sage and I are jet-lagged, he's got stomach flu, and my dislike of crowds is peaking. So thank God for the painting of hermits, because it's my favorite thing in the museum. I like it even more than Fra Angelico's more spectacular and better-known *Coronation of the Virgin* in another room, with its exploding, gilded bursts like rocket fire around Mary's head. The hermits are more my speed. The Desert Fathers and Mothers were, after all, the ones who really rooted Catholicism in people's minds. Abba Poemen, one of the Desert Fathers, once told a disciple not to "give your heart to that which does not satisfy your heart." For a few minutes in the mosh pit of the Uffizi in the company of these hermits, that's what I find: satisfaction.

In a couple of weeks, I will be forty years old. That's part of the reason we're in Italy, but primarily, it seemed necessary to see the bombastic side of Catholicism. It was time to go to the Vatican, to see priests and nuns everywhere rather than once in a blue moon. And there was also the issue of needing to see faith in settings that would remind me of time and scale: the oldest Catholic cathedral in San Francisco was founded in 1854, whereas the church around the corner from the apartment we're renting in Rome's Trastavere neighborhood dates from AD 340. When my Poor Clare friends asked if I was going to Italy on pilgrimage, I asked in turn if it was okay if the pilgrimage included a lot of food and wine. They laughed and said it was. Being Catholic again has revealed that old-school penitence is not really my style, and to be honest, it makes me very cranky.

I still fast during Lent, but I also complain about it; sorry, God, but food makes me happy, and that's why feeding people at the shelter also makes me happy. It's a small thing I can do. I tithe as much money as I can, year-round and more so during Lent and Advent, but not to the diocese or the Bishop's Appeal until my local bishop does something about the molestation cases stacked up on his desk and stops saying ignorant things about women and LGBT people. My tithe goes to the shelter where I volunteer, to the local food bank, to organizations working for progressive reform in the church. Tithing and volunteering, however, don't seem penitential because they feel good—except for the whole waking-up-at-5:00-AM-on-the-weekend-to-cook-eggs part. And there are plenty of chunky priests and nuns in this world, which may be testimony to the fact that even the holiest person falls prey to temptations of the flesh. If there is any place where hedonism and spirituality can be reconciled, I think it's going to be Italy.

Catholics have gone on pilgrimage for thousands of years. It's actually a pre-Christian tradition; back when our ancestors worshipped nature gods, they believed those gods' powers were embedded in particular locations and traveled there to ask for favors. For years, my understanding of pilgrimages was limited to Chaucer's *Canterbury Tales*, a rather bawdy introduction to the idea of people traveling to a holy site. Today, most pilgrims travel in order to ask God for help with something, by visiting the relics of a particular saint, by heading to a place where miracles are supposed to have occurred, or by heading to the Holy Land itself. Rome has been the site of pilgrimages since the very early 200s, since Peter and Paul are both supposedly interred there. Early pilgrims to Rome had a lot more trouble than even a liberal heretic like me will ever have. In the early 200s, Saints Constantine, Victorian, and Zoe were all caught praying at the tomb of Saint Peter and promptly executed by the Romans. This is unlikely to happen today, but reading about it is a helpful reminder that early Christians had it pretty damn rough.

In spite of stories like that, I've wanted to go on pilgrimage since I read about the Camino de Santiago de Compostela route through Northern Spain. Pilgrims there wear a cockle shell for identification and carry a small pilgrim passport, collecting stamps in particular spots along the fifty-mile hiking route, which culminates in a visit to an elaborate cathedral where they give thanks to Saint James. We thought about going to Spain on this trip, especially since Sage is fluent in Spanish, but the biting, harsh winds of winter would have made for a really difficult trip. Also, to be frank, there is no gelato on the Compostella. Nor are there dozens of minute macchiatos to be drunk daily among stylish Italian men. Nor are there consciousness-shattering works of art, plush leather handbags at bargain prices, or piazzas to sit around in and people-watch. Italy it is.

Florence is an excellent place to start looking for the middle ground between pilgrim and pleasure-seeker. The

Christmas lights strung from roof to roof lead the way to my first glimpse of the Duomo, and some combination of jet lag and mental disassociation caused by walking on European soil for the first time in twenty-two years makes me stop on the cobblestones. Maybe it's awe, because the Duomo is fucking awesome. And I think, What have I done to deserve the sight of something this amazing? *Ad majorem Dei gloriam*, as the Jesuits say. For the greater glory of God. Remember that people built the Duomo because they believed. The Italians milling around don't even bother to look up, whereas we and the other tourists have neck aches for days after that first sighting. But after doing a couple of laps around it, we pass through the piazza and emerge on the other side surrounded by the kind of high-end shops I'm terrified to walk into for fear of looking too shabby: Prada, Versace, even a Belstaff store where the leather jackets in the window lead to a rapid series of mental calculations about whether we could go without eating for a month if I bought one.

The New Year's Eve crowds are milling around on the Ponte Vecchio, its cupboard-size shops full of gold and diamonds sealed up tightly for the evening. On the other side of the river, the streets become narrower, harder to navigate, and we find a restaurant at the end of one of them filled with young Italian guys in skintight T-shirts and gold neck chains. Back on the Duomo side, all the major piazzas are being set up for concerts. The guy who runs our apartment, a chubby, ebullient metalhead from our generation, nearly jumped up and down in glee when he found out that Sage is a drummer, and he happily drew us up a map. "Over here we have the 1970s disco," he said that afternoon, while he lit one cigarette from the smoking butt of another, "and over here the classical, and the rock. And over here we have the Godspell." Sage and I glanced at one another, confused. "Godspell?" "Si, the Godspell." The last time I saw *Godspell* was when my older sister's Catholic high school did a production of it back in the late 1970s. All that remains of that experience is the memory of a teenage Jesus in rainbow suspenders and bell-bottoms. Do the Italians have some sort of fetish for cheesy Christian musicals? And why would they be producing this on one of the biggest tourist holidays of the year?

That evening, after purchasing a cone of gelato bigger than my head and managing to eat about half of it before my body threatens sugar shock, we wander around from piazza to piazza. The fact that Italian pop music is beyond terrible is made manifest in the overly emotive balladeering and tinkling synthesizers being pumped through speakers on every street in addition to the live bands. We decide to go find the Godspell just because the novelty of seeing it on New Year's Eve in Florence is too weird to resist.

In the midst of a packed piazza, we find instead a full African American gospel choir in baby-blue robes, complete with a singing pastor and a robed band behind him that includes a middle-aged woman pounding the shit out of the drums. The Italians are clapping along, dancing, throwing their hands in the air. "Ah, he meant Gospel," we both laugh. Even though we've been out of Oakland for less than forty-eight hours, the music makes it feel as if we're right back home. Within a couple of blocks of our house there are no fewer than a dozen African American churches—Baptist, African Methodist Episcopalian, Church of God in Christ, Pentecostal, and a few storefront churches with their own invented denominations, in addition to one of Oakland's African American Catholic churches, with kente-cloth banners hanging from its eaves out front. Oakland is a city with a white minority, and our churches reflect that. I may love my faith, but even the most ardent Catholic has to admit that in contrast to these other churches, most of our music sucks. It is dirgelike, sincere, and dull as dirt. Even on Easter and Christmas, there's little joyful feeling to it. There are only so many Marty Haugen and St. Louis Jesuits tunes a person can take before the shouting, pumping beats and wails of praise coming from the church down the street become irresistible in comparison. Maybe these Catholic Italians feel the same way, because they are certainly getting down.

While it would doubtless be great to stay up and see the fireworks shot from the roof of the Duomo at midnight, Sage's stomach flu is wearing him to shreds, and after fourteen hours of flights—twelve of which were spent behind a very drunk college girl slamming her seat back into my knees—we are barely managing to stay upright. We go back to the hotel, shove in earplugs, and attempt to manage a few hours of sleep.

In the morning the streets are glittering with thousands of shattered bottles, and I crunch my way to the local café, where two cappuccinos go down in quick succession, go back to the hotel, wake Sage, and shower, and we head back to the Duomo for Mass. The temperature in Florence dropped overnight, and it's now in the thirties. The Duomo's massive high ceiling and million-yard nave must make the notion of heating the place a joke, because not only is the priest's breath visible, so is the choir's, and the people around us are constantly rubbing their hands and knees together in a vain effort to keep the circulation up. Poking around the Duomo's website the day before (in keeping with our host's metal obsession, the hotel's WiFi password is a variation on Metallica), I decided it sort of made sense to go to a Latin Mass. After all, isn't that what all those conservative Catholics want to return to?

I've never been to one before; although there is a church in Oakland that does the full, pre-Vatican II Tridentine Mass, friends had implied that my being a tattooed woman with short hair there would probably net me a lot of unfriendly glares. Apparently, the women who go to Tridentine Mass in Oakland wear lace veils on their heads, a practice based on one of Paul's letters that most Catholic women gladly stopped obeying decades ago. But since the Italian Mass is impossible for me to follow, I figured that in Latin I'd at least be able to pick up on the basic bits: Bach's Mass in B Minor has played enough times on my car stereo to help me remember what "kyrie" means, and I did major in classics for a couple of years.

In actuality, I'm totally lost and bored after about fifteen minutes. The only thing keeping me awake is the vision of

Hell painted on the Duomo ceiling, which depicts the pale, rippling flesh of hundreds of naked sinners. They're being judged by a God who looks royally pissed. One sinner, with his legs spread and bits exposed, looks like he's deeply regretting his lack of wardrobe on the Judgment Day. This vision is as colorful as Dante might have imagined it, and if it wasn't there to distract me from the droning priest, the jet lag would have sliced through those two cappuccinos, and like a lot of the elderly people around me, I would have nodded off.

Going to a Latin Mass does nothing more than convince me that Latin Mass is a terrible thing. People who defend it say it preserves the mystery of the Eucharist, but having the priest's back turned to the congregation makes it feel more like it's none of our business. Occasionally, back home, Father Mellow or Father Borough will invite the congregation to stand around the altar with him as he blesses the bread and wine. That feels more appropriate; after all, the earliest Christians celebrated Eucharist together in what they called agape feasts, which literally means "love Mass," and the donuts we chomp together after Mass in contemporary times are a faint echo of that. Doesn't everyone love donuts? The Tridentine tradition of shrouding the host with the priest's back makes that small miracle feel even more distant and remote, as if he's doing card tricks. When I began teaching, one of my mentors gave me a salient piece of advice: "Never turn your back on your students." When the priest in the Duomo turns around and starts the Eucharistic prayer, it feels like all the congregants are being shut out. In my class, everyone would whip out their iPhones and start texting. In the Duomo, people stare up at the ceiling and yawn.

Intimacy between the priest and the congregation must be impossible in a space like this, but that doesn't explain why the Tridentine Mass requires no fewer than six priests in gilded, lacy vestments, male altar servers lofting a six-foot-high golden cross, and a shuffling series of guys parading in behind them who may or may not be seminarians of some sort. There are so many men circling the altar that it looks like a rugby scrum. And yet, as in every other Catholic church I've been to, the pews are full of women. If I were back home, there would at least be female lectors, but in keeping with some of the more macho propensities of Italian culture I've already begun to observe, this Mass looks like a testosterone fest.

When it finally rolls around to the consecration, I'm worried, wondering whether everyone will kneel, but to my relief, everyone remains standing except for one woman in the choir, who presses her denim-clad knees into the icy marble floor, clutches her hands together under her chin, rocks back and forth, and looks like she's about to start weeping. It seems that when Italians aren't yelling at one another—which they seem to constantly do—they are still incapable of holding in their emotions. But there's nothing emotional for me about this service, other than a sense of feeling completely out of place.

Churches in Florence are so elaborate, so full of flourishes and intricate touches, that the cumulative result of walking through several in a day is complete overload. Instead of feeling uplifted, I feel like my eyeballs are going to fall out.

There is no place to rest your gaze in an Italian church—in most of them, the bronzed, gilded, mosaic, frescoed, and carved surfaces obfuscate the altar, the tabernacle, and even the crucifix to the point that it's hard to locate them. In every niche, there is a different statue venerating a different saint or martyr. So used to the more stripped-down American style of church with big windows and lots of light, the dark, murky atmosphere of Italian churches is hard for me to adjust to. And because we're there just after Christmas, every church has a crèche.

Crèches have become a rarity in the United States, but we had one when I was a kid. My dad called it a manger scene, and it was a shoebox-size wooden shack with an open front where we'd arrange plastic figurines of Mary, Joseph, and the Magi. Dad said it was an Irish tradition that we were supposed to stay up late on Christmas Eve and add the baby Jesus figurine to the wee manger, but one year the cat got a hold of little J.C. and batted him around the house until he was lost forever. For some reason I remember replacing Jesus with a wine cork wrapped in a swaddling of Kleenex.

In Italy, the crèches are so elaborate that they look like sets for a community theater production of *Cats*. A few of them have working fountains (with the Holy Family depicted in one at the top of a waterfall, as if they are about to tumble over it), and many have creepy animatronic Magi and even animatronic sheep. Every one of them is loaded with thousands of twinkling lights, gobs of glitter, and hundreds of figurines of people, sheep, donkeys, chickens, and goats.

Some are pocket-size and others are life-size, with full-body mannequins standing around mangers the size of wheelbarrows. There are desert crèches, tropical crèches, Arctic Circle crèches, and even a few that look suspiciously like Vegas. The innate Italian propensity for exuberance and bling is manifest in these manger scenes, and we see hundreds of them in just a few weeks. Something about the aggressively cluttered décor of most Italian churches turns me off, but I do like the crèches. They are so innocent and sweet, like Catholic dollhouses arranged and tended by elderly nuns, whom we sometimes catch dusting the miniature roofs. Soon enough Sage and I start whispering "Crèche!" to one another—which we pronounce like an old-school rapper saying "frrresssshhhh"— whenever we spot a new one.

Reliquaries, also seen in nearly every Italian church, are also a rarity in the States. Back when I was in RCIA, Father Mellow told us that there were some saints' bones embedded in the church's altar, but he also admitted that nobody in the parish was sure which saints they belonged to because that information had gone missing over the years. In Italy, this veneration of bits and pieces of bodies is vivid and gory. Although many of them look like particularly ornate jewelry boxes and it's tough to tell what's inside, others will reveal, upon closer inspection, a shriveled body part. Reliquaries were invented back in medieval times, when people were much more apt to buy into the idea that you might find a shard of the True Cross while crusading your way across the Holy Land, or that a vial of some saint's blood or her finger or toe might actually work miracles. Back then, people believed that the Devil was literally walking among us, and that he was the one causing plagues, wars, and famines rather than human greed and dirty drinking water. The idea that you could actually touch something venerated and full of holiness was a comfort to believers and a tool for conversion of unbelievers. I try to imagine this working on some of my atheist friends as I stare at the heart of some obscure saint, which looks like beef jerky. Florence is teeming with reliquaries. With all the money the Medicis were throwing around, they could afford to import and gild lots of bones and fleshy bits, many of them stolen from freshly dug graves. Some reliquaries aren't so gory; as I soon discover, there are miraculous paintings as well.

One cold evening, we duck into what looks from the outside like a particularly plain church on a piazza near our hotel. Just to the left of the door at the back of the nave, there's a corner shrine stuffed full of dried and half-dead flowers, surrounded by more dripping candles than I've seen in any other church. The shrine is built around a smallish painting of the annunciation, the moment when the Angel of the Lord arrived to tell Mary she was going to bear God's child, which must have been particularly popular during the Renaissance, because there are enough annunciations in Florence to crowd out the rest of the New Testament. This one depicts the angel sending what look like golden threads toward Mary's belly, and an elderly man is just getting up from kneeling in front of it when I walk up.

On the walls surrounding the painting are hundreds of what I've always heard referred to as "milagros": tin plates pressed in the shape of body parts, or sacred hearts, or animals. In Mexico, you see these everywhere, usually left as altar gifts when a saint has worked a particular miracle for someone. If you have a sick heart, you leave a heart milagro and pray for help with that; if you break your arm, you leave an arm. I'd never seen one in Italy before, but here in the Santissima Annunziata, there are so many that they are layered one on top of another. They are old and tarnished-looking, rust creeping along their edges, and one catches my eye: it's over a foot long, in the shape of an old sailing ship. Some Italian sailors must have pinned it there hundreds of years ago, before they embarked on a long voyage.

We do a couple of laps around the church, which is having a vespers service, chants and prayers echoing through the aisles, but I keep circling back to the shrine. There is something that pulls me back there, something about the layers of milagros, the glittering strings connecting the angel to Mary that feels so primitive, a kind of expression of faith in the mystic side of Catholicism that has almost been hidden beyond recognition in most of the United States. You're more likely to see this kind of thing in East Oakland, with its Chicano/Latino population carrying the Virgen de Guadalupe down the streets, or at Mission Dolores in San Francisco, where they rain rose petals down on the congregation on her feast day. Guadalupe is venerated for many reasons, but a primary one is because she's La Morequita—the little brown one, a mestiza who actually looks like Juan Diego, the indigenous guy who discovered her. He found her on a hill that was formerly a shrine to the indigenous goddess Tonantzin, and that example of *mestizaje*, the blending of primitive mysticism with Christianity, is the only thing I personally know of that's like this Florentine shrine.

I try to puzzle through the brochures and discover that the painting dates to the 1200s, when a Servite monk began it, but he worried it was not beautiful enough, so he abandoned it. When he went to sleep that night, an angel came and completed the painting. Total bullshit, right? Maybe. But this painting has been venerated by pilgrims for eight hundred years. The flowers are from brides-to-be, who leave their bouquets here hoping for a happy marriage. And as I'm standing there, women and men come and light candles, say a quick prayer, drop a euro into a box. Maybe there is something to it, I think, dig out a euro of my own, light a candle, and say a quick prayer for a friend who just got married. She's Jewish, but so was Mary, after all.

Outside, the piazza is filled with milling crowds as usual, and as we go in search of somewhere to eat, we pass a Carabinieri buying lottery tickets from a vending machine embedded into a wall. A few meters from that, there's a Durex machine, and a cigarette machine. "Hold up," I say to Sage, and look back at the condom machine, and up, and there's the Duomo. Just meters from one of the most famous cathedrals in the world, you can buy a jimmy hat 24/7.

It occurs to me that most of the Italian women we've seen are not pushing strollers or holding the hands of small kids. With their big hair and tight jeans, fur coats, heavy makeup, and gold jewelry, Florentine women look way too glamorous to bear children. The truth is that Italians have one of the lowest birthrates in the industrialized world. Twenty-five percent of Italian women never have kids, and twenty-five percent more only have one child. Part of this is economics: the unemployment rate in Italy is staggeringly high for young women, nearly thirty percent at the time of our visit. But a bigger part may be the strong-headedness of Italian women. Just a few days of observing them striding across the cobblestones in skyscraper heels, driving their Vespas at terrifying speeds through Florence's labyrinthine streets, and shouting at their boyfriends between make-out sessions makes it clear that Italian women are not to be fucked with. Italy's culture is so overwhelmingly macho that maybe holding onto control of their fertility is one way in which these tough, recalcitrant Italian women are able to push back against the testosterone wave. I'd come here expecting to see textbook good Catholic women, and found instead Catholic women just like me.

Father Mellow likes to tell a joke about Italian Catholics. A guy goes to confession and the priest asks if he regularly attends Mass. "Si, father," the guy says, "I go to Mass all the time." "How often is that?" the priest asks. "Oh, once or twice a year." Italians seem to epitomize the phrase "cultural

Catholic." They do go to Mass—most of the Masses I hit in Italy are fairly crowded—but as a friend who lived in Rome for many years told me, "They might not necessarily go unless they have a favor to ask." They believe in God, in Jesus and the Spirit and the saints, but they don't get hung up on Vatican dogma, perhaps because it's being issued from their own backyard.

The Catholic guilt so frequently joked about by Americans seems not to be an issue for Italians. This casual version of faith is in direct opposition to the one experienced by my Irish forebears, who got caught up in a version of Catholicism called Jansenism that swept Ireland back in the 1600s. Jansenism was a theology that emphasized sin, predestination, and human depravity over grace, acts of mercy, and forgiveness. This explains a lot about why Irish Catholics, at least in the early days of the great migration, tended to be a lot more pious than their Italian neighbors. My father and grandfathers all grew up in this bleaker kind of Catholic church, and I wonder to this day if much of Dad's attachment to the church was not born out of affection for it as mine was, but out of fear for his mortal soul.

My soul is feeling pretty good in Florence, and my rapidly expanding gut is keeping good company with it. If Italian Catholicism is all about obeying your conscience over following marching orders, that's what I've managed to do so far in addition to gawking at art and eating some impressively massive and delicious meals. But it's time to go where the Church began, back when Catholics prayed in underground churches and Catholicism was something small, humble, free-form, and new.

The Roman neighborhood of Trastevere, like swaths of Oakland, is a former working-class neighborhood slowly gentrifying, and the streets around us are packed with cafés, restaurants, and boutiques. When we step out of our apartment that first evening, the piazza is packed with people drinking beer and wine; there's a woman playing an accordion and another woman doing a fire-eating routine; and there are torches burning outside a restaurant, Carabinieri standing around looking bored, people dropping cones of gelato and shrieking, shattering glass, and Vespas constantly shooting by. Within a few seconds, I nearly get hit by one, step in a pile of dogshit, and collide with several pushy Italian pedestrians. Welcome to Rome.

I haven't kept a journal since high school, but I do occasionally scribble something in my day planner, and on the second day in Rome these words appear: *dirty, noisy, crowded, entertaining.* For the city purported to be the highest seat of the Catholic Church, Rome isn't exactly tranquil or spiritually uplifting. Crossing the street feels like Darwinism in action. The noise is deafening everywhere you go, and it's not just the constantly yelling Italians: it's the scraping, grinding, tearing noise of an ancient city pushed past its limits of capacity, and then compressed down onto itself.

We suddenly come across an architectural dig, right in the middle of a crazy intersection. A hole in the ground has been widened and deepened, and bits of ancient Roman construction poke out of the dirt. As Sage puts it, Roman architecture is "like the old next to the really old." And on top of the old are the people, so very many people. Every time I go to Manhattan, I experience a kind of out-of-body sense of disassociation due to the pushing and shoving crowds, a feeling that if I fell in the street, nobody would bother to stop and pull me up. In Rome, it's more like a pervasive sense of panic that one of the cars driving *on the sidewalk* will mow me down. "Vaffanculo!" Although I have no gift for languages, I did learn to say "fuck you" in Rome. Really, it was a matter of necessity after all the times when I was nearly killed by one of those cute little Italian cars. At the end of every day, I say a prayer of thanks for my survival. Every day, Rome kicks my ass.

But whenever the sensory oversaturation of Rome threatens to overwhelm us, there is always some church to go into for a few minutes of quiet respite. And in many of those churches, there's a Giotto painting, or a Bernini statue, just casually stuck on the side of a shadowy altar. The horrible Italian economy means many Roman churches can't afford to leave the lights on. It takes a few visits before we discover that most of them have installed small boxes where you drop in a euro and the lights come blazing on for five minutes. In many churches, this also triggers a blast of recorded organ music. In a few others, it includes a light show with flashing spotlights on particular works of art or ceiling murals. You stick your euro in the box, the lights and music come on, and you race around as quickly as you can, trying to take in all the reliquaries of shriveled body bits, layers of gilding, paintings, statuary, and knickknacks before the lights and music abruptly turn off. At some point we went through so many of these church light shows that I began expecting them to throw in a laser show or a line of high-kicking priests. Alas, neither of those materialized.

Before we left home, I had attempted to get back in touch with the Italian, who had been moved from his job teaching high school in Sicily to a different job training seminarians in Naples. The Italian told me to get in touch via email when we arrived, but whenever I go into the hipster cafe around the corner from our apartment to check email, there's no reply from him. "I'm sorry you might not see your hot priest friend," Sage jokes as we lean on the counter of yet another café, pounding the macchiatos that are essential to Roman survival. It's a running joke between us that my real mission in coming to Italy was in hoping to finally see some hot priests, because the ones in the States seem to all be well over the AARP line. And in some ways that's better, because there are no confusing crushes to be had, except for intellectual and spiritual ones. But it does rob me of seeing those priests my friend Elizabeth calls "Father What a Waste."

Even if I can't track down the Italian, I want to visit the Chiesa del Gesu, the mother church of the Jesuits, where Saint Ignatius is interred. The Italian had told me that in contrast to the impoverished, short-statured guy who founded the Jesuit order, the Gesu is over-the-top pre-baroque and ridiculously blinged out. Walking in, I can almost imagine Elvis living comfortably there. The ceiling alone is famous; a nearly 3D fresco that is so lifelike it looks like its clouds are creeping down into the church. A group of nuns wanders in just after us, and they are so awed by it that they all look like they're about to tip over backward.

Ignatius's remains are in a side altar dominated by massive gilded whirligig pillars and a huge painting depicting the tiny, balding Spanish saint touching the finger of Jesus. A golden box houses his remains. Thinking back on reading Igantius's autobiography and recounting the stories of him renouncing all worldly goods, the site of this altar makes me cringe. Ignatius would have hated this. Nonetheless, I stop to say a little prayer of thanks, since Ignatius was one of the guys who got my foot in the door of Catholicism back when I was in spiritual direction with the Italian, and when I'm done, Sage nudges me. "I think we found your hot priest," he whispers, and I look over and see a young guy in clericals kneeling in front of the tomb.

He's not hot; he's exquisite: dark eyelashes, high cheekbones, a refined nose, wavy black hair. And he's so deep in prayer that the expression on his face is a half smile of some sort of gratitude. If a guy like that back in the United States decided to enter the priesthood, every woman and man in his acquaintance with a pulse would try to talk him out of it. They'd probably cling to his ankles as he walked up the seminary stairs. Father What a Waste indeed.

It takes us a while to get to the Vatican. Rome is distracting, and we deliberately arrived without an itinerary, knowing there would always be something to do. But after a few days, I feel like it can't be put off any longer, and we head up to Saint Peter's, walking alongside the Tiber, its surface swollen and glassy in the January sun. Thinking of going to the Vatican makes me feel strangely jittery: Will I finally be struck down by the hand of God? Will Benedict be there, and, if so, will I really give him the finger? And what would the Swiss Guards do if I did give him the finger? While pondering this line of thought, we turn a corner and Sage says, "Okay, we're here."

I look up and my first reaction is disappointment. It looks . . . small. Maybe because Saint Peter's square has been inflated in my mind for so long, or because photographs taken from above make it look bigger, but the famous colonnades that people compare to embracing arms and the domes of the basilica behind them are not on the scale I expected. I was expecting the thing to be colossal, mind-blowing, ginormous. In reality, it's just biggish. Though it's early in the morning, the square is teeming with pilgrims, tourists, priests, nuns, even an African cardinal dashing along with his retinue behind him. He stops a few times to strike a pose for tourists' cameras. We get into a queue to pass through metal detectors to enter the basilica, and I remove my studded belt only to find my pants threatening to fall down, which might be appropriate for a sinner: bare-assed before God.

Inside it looks bigger than it does from the outside, but it still feels packed with people, Uffizi-style. The difference is that looking across the length of the church, the people appear to be tiny. And then it occurs to me that this church is actually massive. The Pieta is surrounded by so many people that it's impossible to get within forty feet of it, and it's behind glass anyway, so it mostly looks like staccato flashes of camera lights. Packs of people are crammed in front of every tomb, icon, and pillar, and there are thousands and thousands of works of art, including an elaborately tiled floor and a frescoed ceiling so dizzying it's impossible to rest my eyes on any one part of it.

Another line of people emerges in front of a what looks like a very old metal statue. Sage recognizes it before I do. "See the feet?" he says, and I look, and the saint's toes have been entirely worn off from the hands of pilgrims throughout the centuries. It's a ritual of pilgrimage, one that supposedly gains blessings. "Okay, I have to do this," I say, and I walk by and give each of Peter's feet a swipe, and then remember that thousands of people have done the same thing today, and douse my hands with Purell. God may have healed much of my anxiety, but I'm still a germaphobe.

The tomb of John XXIII is the only place in the basilica where I really want to stop and pray, so I do, in front of his effigy, which showcases his rather impressive gut and promi-nent nose. John was the architect of Vatican II, the guy who said it was time to "shake off the dust that has collected on the throne of St. Peter." When he was a bishop and Pope Pius XII was not doing enough to help Jews during the Hol-ocaust, John fought to protect them. He was a pope who visited prisoners, engaged in dialogue with people from other faiths, and snuck out of the Vatican late at night to walk the streets of Rome. Without John, we'd still be stuck with the Latin Mass. And I would have never returned to the Church, because I would not want to come back to a Church where the priest turned his back on me and my agnostic spouse was viewed as damned. So I stop and close my eyes. *Please, we need another one of you, preferably female.* When I open my eyes, there's a woman sitting next to me. We exchange shy smiles, and I wonder if we're praying for the same thing.

John Paul II's tomb is downstairs, but I walk by it swiftly, only pausing a bit to wonder why there are way more pilgrims here than in front of John XXIII. Maybe it's because he was pope for so freaking long, longer than any pope in centuries. But John Paul II was also the source of most of the coverups of sexual abuse; the groomer of Benedict and all the other ultra-conservative types who run the show these days; and, according to a few sources I've read, kind of a grouch, perfunctory with strangers and dismissive of issues like women's ordination and gay rights. Not to mention the part he played in suppressing Liberation Theology, the movement that began in Central America, which advocates raising the poor from unjust political and social circumstances. The world may have seen him as a grandfatherly type, but he made more than a few mistakes that will take decades to untangle.

Leaving the basilica after an hour or so, we take a few minutes to sit in Saint Peter's square and watch the hordes in the winter sun. A young woman is doing yoga as her male friend snaps photo after photo. Teenagers are talking on cell phones, babies crying, pigeons shitting on the cobblestones, Swiss Guards being stoic as people point at them and laugh. And that's when I realize that the Vatican is Disneyland for Catholics. There are Vatican gift shops and the Vatican post office and Vatican roach coaches selling hot dogs and chips. Around the corner is the entrance to Vatican City, which is surrounded by towering walls and off-limits to pilgrims and tourists; I watch for a minute as limousines drive in and out through its gate. This is not where I'm going to find the true Church. I come closer to the true Church sitting around with my friends, cooking eggs for homeless women, sitting in a pew back home, lying on my couch reading Psalms. I came closer to the Church in my talks with the Italian priest too, conversations I wouldn't mind starting up again, but by the time I finally get an email from him, Sage and I are about to leave Rome and have only a few days left on the trip. There's no way we'll make it to Naples. It might have been a nice change after the Vatican. There is too much pomp in Rome to make it seem even remotely close to the life Jesus led. The Vatican is admittedly beautiful and majestic, but it's not about the real hard work of belief.

Back in Trastevere, I've been sleeping with earplugs in, not only because of the street noise but also because the church in the piazza around the corner rings its bells four times an hour, every hour, all night long. The penultimate day we're in Rome, we finally go into it, and I find yet another surprise. Santa Maria in Trastevere is one of the oldest churches in

Rome; its foundations were laid in the 300s. It may have been the first church in Rome where Christians openly celebrated Eucharist. On the outside, there is a mosaic of Mary holding an infant Christ, surrounded by ten women holding lamps. Inside, the church glitters; the dome above the altar is also covered in mosaics, and they are stunning. I suddenly think of Yeats's "Sailing to Byzantium," which I stayed up all night attempting to memorize during college, images of mosaics floating away between bong hits. "Shit, we should have come earlier," I tell Sage. I mean, come on, it's a church with a ton of women on the front, just yards from where we've been staying. They might as well have hung a neon sign out front with my name on it. But some things take a while to fully reveal themselves, something every believer knows.

In the little gift shop, I'm buying a package of postcards of those mosaics, when the clerk starts rapidly talking to me in Italian. I point to Sage, who doesn't speak Italian either but has been able to get us around with his Spanish. The clerk tells him to tell the *donna* to go back into the church and look at one mosaic in particular because it's *uniquo*, and he acts it out for us so we won't miss it and then looks back at me. "Uniquo," he says. "Si, grazie," I reply, nodding.

Back inside, I find it immediately. How did I miss this? I have missed so many things. It takes a stubborn guy to help me see the *uniquo*, in this case, a mosaic of Jesus with Mary, only he is not an infant being held by her. He is a man, and they are standing side by side, and he has his arm around her shoulders, as the clerk acted out. Jesus and Mary are adults.

The same height, the same facial expressions. Here, in this place, in this mosaic pieced together nearly a thousand years ago, they are equal.

Assisi is in the Umbrian hills, a landscape of rolling peaks and golden fields sprouting olive trees and teetering cone-shaped Italian cypress. There are lots and lots of sheep, picturesquely chomping away. Assisi's train station looks pretty down-at-heel, so my expectations of what we'll find are low until I follow my husband's pointing finger and look up. What looks like an enchanted castle juts out from a nearby hill. And like a fairytale castle, it's sugar-frosting pink. A quirk of local geology resulted in pink granite that stonemasons quarried from nearby Mount Subasio, so Assisi's walls, streets, and churches look like tic-tac-toe boards made from pink and gray stones. From the bottom of the hill, the entire town glows. It's so beautiful, and so unexpectedly beautiful, that I suspect it may be a fake.

We squeeze onto a bus crammed with the members of a local scouting troop, hormonal Italian preteen boys and girls amped up on outdoor exercise laughing and shouting all the way up the very steep hill into town. When we finally wind up at the top, we squeeze off and head downhill into the twisting maze of Assisi streets, most of them so steep they're terraced with staircases. We're booked into a cheap hotel with an airplane-sized bathroom. But even this place has a surprise. "Watch this," Sage says, opening the shutters and revealing a stunning view sweeping over the rooftops and flowering backyard gardens and up to the Rocca Maggiore, a crumbling medieval fortress that overlooks the town. "Welcome to Italy," he says with a laugh.

The entire town slopes downward at a steep angle, and as we walk out to explore, that angle pulls us through town, past the San Rufino cathedral, past the Basilica of Santa Chiara, as Saint Clare is called here, and farther on down through streets so narrow they're impassable even by miniature Italian cars to the massive Basilica of San Francesco. The slope seems to be pulling us that way, so I figure on our first evening here, we might as well visit Saint Francis.

Outside the basilica there is yet another crèche. As it turns out, the crèche was invented by Francis himself, so Assisi celebrates that every year by holding a crèche competition. There are over a hundred window crèches all over town, including my favorite, one in a restaurant window made out of potatoes, but the one at the basilica is yet another life-sized model with an oversized papier-mâché camel in addition to the usual assortment of papier-mâché people. And there are friars and Poor Clares *everywhere*. I saw priests and nuns in Florence and Rome, but nowhere near this many of them, and the tininess of the town makes it seem like they run the place, which they effectively do.

Franciscan garb is distinctive and hasn't changed in almost a thousand years: a rough-spun brown robe with a cowl neck and a rope belt around the waist. The Clares wear a variation on this same outfit, some with a brown veil, some without. Franciscans are discalced, meaning they don't wear closed-toed shoes (a few of the cloistered orders go totally barefoot year-round), so all the friars and nuns are wearing sandals with thick woolen socks, a look not usually seen on anyone but German tourists waiting for cable cars in San Francisco. One young friar is strumming a guitar and leading a group of teenage Italian pilgrims standing in a circle in an upbeat version of Francis's "Canticle of the Sun," a sung prayer that's reproduced on napkins, greeting cards, and wooden plaques in the tourist shops all over town. The teenagers don't look bored or disdainful; a few actually have their eyes closed, and they're all smiling and singing together. Like the sugar-pink, sparkly surface of Assisi itself, it's almost too sweet of a sight for my cynical American gaze to bear.

Once we enter the basilica, something pulls me past the people gawking at the frescoes, through the upper church, and then through the lower church. It almost feels as if I'm suddenly in a hurry to get somewhere, but I don't know why or where until we arrive at the very lowest level of the structure: the crypt. Normally this is not where I would want to go. All those preserved fingers and toes in Florence might have been enough to put me off looking at reliquaries forever, but Francis's tomb is different.

When he died, young and in severe pain from lifelong illnesses and working so hard, often going without food and drink on behalf of the poor, one of the Franciscan brothers buried his body in a hidden place so that Francis's bones would not be stolen and scattered like those of so many other saints. He would be kept whole in this tiny town where he was born. When the crypt was excavated in the 1800s, a simple stone tomb was built, carved out of the same pink stone as the basilica's walls. The crypt is dark, and SILENCIO signs posted everywhere are working their magic even on the never silent Italians. We squeeze onto one of the benches to sit as waves of pilgrims and tourists pass by.

I close my eyes, thinking that just for a moment, I'll try to say a fast prayer and then we can go back upstairs and look at those frescoes, but my eyes stay shut of their own accord. Shuffling feet and the occasional whisper are the only sound. This isn't sleep, but it isn't my typical state of agitated awareness either. Back home, I cannot meditate for any prolonged amount of time, but in the crypt, it only takes a couple of minutes before my shoulders relax and my hands stop twisting. "Don't fight it," someone says in my mind, and it's the voice of the Italian back in Berkeley; it's the voice of Father Mellow during Mass; it's the voice of my friends and the people who love me, believers and not. *Don't fight it. Don't resist.* The next thing I'm aware of is Sage passing me a tissue, because I've apparently begun to weep, and I open my eyes and understand that these aren't my usual rage or misery tears. Being this close to what remains of Francis has resulted in a wave of joy. It feels like God's stepped in to say, "Hey, lady, I'm here. I've always been here."

Finally, we get up and circle the tomb. On its back side, people have shoved photos of loved ones through slots in the grate, young and old faces alike piling up against the stone. Off to one side, a friar is filling out requests for Masses to be said in the crypt. I pull out some euros, hand them to the friar as an offering, write down the name of a friend going through chemo for breast cancer on the slip proffered by the friar, who hands me back a receipt, which breaks the spell a little when I realize that this is the first time anyone's ever handed me a receipt in a church. Sage and I climb the stairs, back up to the upper levels, and we stand silently for a while looking at the frescoes that depict Francis's life in all its stages, from his vision of Christ at San Damiano, to his renunciation of a life of wealth and leisure, to his preaching to the birds and embracing the leper, to his tonsuring Clare, to his decline and death. Many of the frescoes were damaged in the huge earthquake that hit Assisi in the 1990s. Some pieces were reduced to the size of grains of sand, and a few of the images have huge gaping cracks running through them. But most look just as they did when they were painted. Francis was short and slight. His eyebrows seem to have come together just above his nose.

Outside the sun is setting over the valley in yet another explosion of pink, and Sage asks if I am okay. "What happened in there?" he says with some concern, and I can't really answer. I vaguely gesture toward the sunset, toward the singing friar, toward the crèche, and tell him the truth. I don't know what happened, but I know that right now, I am really, really happy. To be here with him, lucky enough to be here at all. Ignatius called this the gift of tears, being surprised by joy, finding God in all things. To this agnostic's eternal credit, he just nods. And we watch the sunset for a while together, believer and questioner, and then walk together back up the steep hill.

EPILOGUE

EPILOGUE

Toward the end of her life, Dorothy Day, the socialist-anarchist writer turned founder of the Catholic Worker movement, attempted to explain what she thought young people who joined the Worker would gain from it. "They learn not only to love, with compassion," she wrote, "but to overcome fear." It's Dorothy's admonition that we should not be afraid, that we need to work together, that the answer to loneliness is love, and that "love comes with community" that I'm thinking of this evening as a room in my parish fills up with women.

When I began RCIA, it was Dorothy Day's life that showed me it is possible for a woman to move from a radical life in the secular world to one of radical faith. And even now, that message sticks as I begin this new work of bringing people together to listen to their stories of faith. For months, the pray-and-bitch ladies and I have been planning a series of sessions on women's spirituality, and as the gears began turning, we met one woman who is leaving a tenured professorial gig to become a hospital chaplain, and another who retired from her work for the diocese and now counsels prisoners at San Quentin. Their sense of vocation is humbling. But in spite of how busy they are, they pitched in to help with the planning, and tonight we begin.

While I was grateful to return to my church after Italy and actually be able to understand what the priests were saying during Mass, I now have a sense of an even deeper schism between the American bishops and their flock, one that seems to be growing wider every day. The Vatican is getting ready to shift us over to a new missal, the text we follow during Mass, which hews closer to the Latin now and contains verbally garbled phrasings like "consubstantial with the father." The new translation forces us not to respond to the priest's "Peace be with you" by saying "And also with you," but by saying "And with your spirit," which just sounds lame. One elderly guy in my parish complains that these petty changes make him feel like he's being treated like a child. "If someone says 'Peace be with you' to me," he says, "I'm saying 'And also with you' and I don't care if the bishop's a lip reader."

But there are even more serious rumblings in the pews about things heavier than the new missal. A 2011 study by the Guttmacher Institute revealed that ninety-eight percent of American Catholic women freely admit that they use some form of birth control. So much for the "natural family planning" the cardinals have been trying to get us to use.

And another poll by the Public Religion Research Institute indicated that more than seventy-five percent of practicing Catholics support gay marriage and civil unions, a higher percentage than even some of the more liberal Protestant denominations, and even more evidence of how out of touch with the people the hierarchy really is. On June 24, 2011, the Catholic governor of New York signed gay marriage into law. Edwin O'Brien, the archbishop of Baltimore, gets quoted talking about this on my Facebook feed: "It seems overnight we've lost the community on opposition to gay marriage," he says. No shit, dude.

These schisms make me think about what it means to have a vocation. Not that I want to be a priest; as much as I want to see women in that role, it's not for me. I'm loath to give up teaching and writing to devote myself full time to the spiritual care of others—although, arguably, teaching and writing might someday be a form of that. Even though my job exhausts me, over the last few years I've come to appreciate it more, to be grateful for my funny, smart students and the colleagues I work with who are also writers, all of us trying to teach people how to string words together so they can make sense of the world. Even though I have an army of fellow believers on my side, always pushing me to find new ways to think about faith, part of this new Catholic version of me still feels lost.

I'm still searching for a sense of what my calling really means in terms of service to others. My writing will always be too profane to be "Catholic" enough for many of my fellow believers. Speaking in churches will never be more than an occasional thing and could be taken away at any time if enough of those conservative bloggers keep stirring up crap about it.

Thinking I might return to study, I spend a day at the Jesuit School of Theology, sitting in on classes with young seminarians and one very outspoken young nun. It makes me miss being a student, but after spending a decade paying off loans from my first graduate degree, quitting my job to get another one seems risky. When I tell the dean of students that I would like to keep my job at least part time while attending, she frowns. "You won't be part of the community if you do that," she warns. I'm tired of being told I can't be part of a community. People told me that for years before I came back to the Church, and somehow, I discovered one anyway.

It takes conversations with the prayer ladies and my new spiritual director, a tough-talking nun, to understand that for now, my vocation may just mean sitting with other Catholic agitators and hearing what we have to say about what the Church could and should be. If ninety-eight percent of us use birth control and seventy-five percent are in favor of gay marriage, even if those poll numbers are somewhat skewed, we are really a majority. The more vocal minority of conservative Catholics is just a hell of a lot louder. Perhaps there's a way to work together to better express what we think, and that's what sparked this newer, bigger gathering.

At the parish I sit with Agnes and Sophia and watch the door as women come in, more of them than we expect, shaking off the rain and complaining about how cold the room is and laughing and talking, talking, talking. I have known since I was a little girl that when you put a bunch of women together in a room, you're going to get a deafening roar going within minutes. Margaret finally gets everyone quiet, gathering us around for a prayer, and then Agnes talks for a while about Saint Clare and relational energy as a way of seeing God, and then she gives everyone some questions about why they stay Catholic and breaks us into groups for further conversation.

I start counting heads. There are more than forty women in the room—way more than we planned for, so we have to keep leaving the room to find more chairs. As usual, I seem to be the youngest by decades, but that's okay; somebody has to be strong enough to heft all those chairs. For years now I have looked around for another tattooed rebel Catholic girl during Mass, but I've yet to spot her. If I did, it might be kind of freaky anyway, like bumping into a forgotten twin. If my generation has really and truly decided to reject religion, it's unlikely I'll ever discover a peer in this Church. And that's okay too; secular friends my age have mostly come to accept my being Catholic as yet another odd piece of who I am. Some have even asked me to write about it for their magazines. Others have come to churches when I'm giving a talk. But let's just say that it's still not a topic I bring up at parties. My spiritual soul mates, as it turns out, aren't necessarily people exactly like me; rather, they're people I want to learn from.

There are quite a few of them in this room tonight telling their stories. Do we talk about feeling neglected and rejected by the Church? Yes. Do we bash a bishop or two, talk a little trash about the Vatican, moan about a priest who said something dumb about women or gays or both? Sure. But mostly, we talk about what faith does for us, how it moves us through life with an awareness of other people's suffering and drives us to do something about that suffering. It reminds me of a conversation I had with Father Mellow, way back on the first night I spoke to him. "The Church is both sinner and holy," he said. "So are all of us."

During Lent, I go to a talk on the Psalms, because that's one of the things I do for fun on my nights off these days. The woman leading the talk is a theology professor, and she tells us that many of the Psalms—the sung poem-prayers that make up the longest book of the Old Testament—don't take the form of praise but the form of a lament or even a curse. The Psalmists will cry to God for help and then issue a complaint about God or about his or her enemy. They will then make a confession that they trust God will act and end with a vow of praise. "It seems to go against Jesus' teachings," she tells us, "the whole Catholic ethic of social justice."

But what these curses gave the Hebrews was a sense of catharsis. It takes our negative sentiments and gives them to God, so we're less likely to act on them. And if you believe at the end of such a prayer that God still won't turn you away, that becomes an act of confidence and a real transformation. What Christ—who prayed the Psalms himself—asks us to do, she says, is to really experience a change of heart: a metanoia. This word is often defined as "repentance," but it means something greater. It is a transformation, a conversion, a realization that God will not reject you. To experience a metanoia means that you understand what the Psalmists knew: you may curse and bewail your state and the state of the world around you, but in doing so you may also get closer to God.

In my years as a returned Catholic, I've learned that it's impossible to arrive at a metanoia alone. Yes, there is a role for the priests, bishops, and popes who run the show, but ultimately, living a life of faith is not about following marching orders. It's about finding God in other people, feeling the movement of the Spirit, living the compassion of Christ as best we can. There is a reason Catholics return again and again to the idea of conscience, that deep, secretive part of ourselves that secular life makes it easy to ignore. A neglected conscience will shrivel and curl into itself in a manner that can feel impossible to unfold. But it will unfold with the help of others. It will grow. Mine does, every day.

Faith is part of my identity, and it's not going away, even if it's not always a perfect fit. Maybe the sense of rebellion felt by those of us who envision a better version of the Church is the same as the anger the Psalmists expressed. A better version of the Church, after all, is where we will ultimately

find a better version of ourselves. All the saints whose exam-
ples I follow—alive and dead, believers and not, secular and
holy—are agitators for reinvention: of the Church, the self,
the world. And they never give up. We are all ready for a
metanoia. Maybe we have already seen it begin.

ACKNOWLEDGMENTS

Thanks are owed to the following people.

To the pray-and-bitch ladies, the women's group, my spiritual directors, and the priests and nuns who put up with believers like me. You'll go unnamed here, but not unloved.

To the people who opened the door at the beginning of this journey, and to the people who manage to keep it propped open as the journey goes on.

To my family: Mom, Betsy, Robert, Christine, Vicki, Ava, Lior, Melanie, Jennifer, Avi, and all of my in-laws. To the family members who are no longer with us here on the ground. Also to extended family member Jerry for loaning me Merton's *The Sign of Jonas*, and to my godfather Robert.

To my secular posse. Special thanks to the former Kitchen Sinkers: Carla, Elka, Stefanie, Jen, Nicole, and Jeff. To Ross for the tattoos. To the Royal Coffee crew (it will be Royal forever). To Lisa and Erin. To the Saint Mary's crew and the Cal Shakes crew. And to Sam, always the best.

To my colleagues at Berkeley, especially the writers who know the dark circles under the eyes and carpal tunnel that come from practicing what we preach. Many extra thanks, as always, to Jane.

To my writing teachers, and to the writers who are my teachers.

To my students, with special gratitude to the 110 and 130 students who put up with hearing excerpts from this book in progress and gave me great advice.

To all the readers who wrote me kind notes after my last book was published, came to readings, and helped me understand that I was not writing into a void.

To my local bookstores and their staffers, especially Carlo and Mary at Sagrada Sacred Arts and the entire staff at Moe's. Also to the librarians at the Graduate Theological Union and at UC Berkeley: I promise I'll return everything soon.

To the guests and staff at the women's shelter, and to my fellow 5 A.M. volunteers.

To the people at Farley's, where many swaths of this book were written.

To my neighbors in the Triangle.

To my wonderful agent Michelle, for supporting this book from beginning to end, and for having a great sense of humor.

To my equally wonderful editor Roxy, whose careful, compassionate feedback elevated this book beyond what I ever thought it could be.

Thanks to Elke Barter for the cover, Beth Partin for copy edits, and to Jack Shoemaker, Kelly Winton, Liz Parker, Julia Kent, and everyone else at Counterpoint.

And finally, to Sage, who is brave enough to be a questioner. This book is dedicated to all my fellow heretics.

ABOUT THE AUTHOR

Kaya Oakes is the author of *Slanted and Enchanted: The Evolution of Indie Culture*, the poetry collection *Telegraph*, and cofounder of *Kitchen Sink*, winner of the Utne Independent Press Award for Best New Magazine. She teaches writing at the University of California, Berkeley, and lives in Oakland. Her website is http://www.oakestown.org.